Tennesse

Ad

A collection of trails from Memphis to the Great Smoky Mountains

David A. Moore

Big Air Publishing
102 English Court
Hendersonville, TN 37075

 ISBN 0-9643399-0-0.

INTRODUCTION

Tennesseans, be thankful for such a great state in which to live and ride. We can experience everything from the bottom lands of the west, the Cumberland Plateau running up the middle of our state, and the Great Smokies that give us the chance to climb 6,000-foot mountains. Everywhere in between you'll find hundreds of miles of trails to lead you to waterfalls, white water rivers, deep clean lakes, scenic gorges, and a variety of wildlife. I've been very fortunate to travel throughout Tennessee and had the time to see it from atop my bike. The following pages describe some of the most popular trails as well as many you may not have heard about. Tennessee has a lot of land available to us. Go out and explore this great state of ours.

To the best of my knowledge, all of these trails are currently open. This doesn't mean they will be forever; that's up to you. Trail closures occur for two main reasons: We make other user groups mad, and we are destructive to sensitive areas. We need to be aware that it's up to us and take appropriate action. **YIELD TO HORSES AND HIKERS.**

I strongly suggest that you join a local bike club, IMBA, or NORBA. These groups' main focus is to keep existing trails open and to open areas that are currently closed to cyclists. You'll also meet others to ride with and discover new places to ride.

Take the initiative to keep your trails in good shape. For every four hours you ride, invest one hour into the trails. Work on improving what you have, expand new trails, or clean up the area. It's up to all of us.

Mountain biking is dangerous. Use common sense and good judgment on all trails. Many of these areas are highly technical and caution should be used. Don't ride past your ability level. For safety, ride with a friend. **ALWAYS WEAR A HELMET.**

BEFORE YOU RIDE, READ

I hope everyone who reads this book will take time to learn IMBA's Rules of the Trail and practice these measures each time you ride.

1. **RIDE ON OPEN TRAILS ONLY.** Respect trail and road closures (ask if unsure), avoid possible trespass on private land, and obtain permits and authorization as may be required. Federal and state wilderness areas are closed to cycling. Additional trails may be closed because of sensitive environmental concerns or conflicts with other users. Your riding example will determine what is closed to all cyclists!

2. **LEAVE NO TRACE.** Be sensitive to the dirt beneath you. You should not ride even on open trails under conditions where you will leave evidence of your passing, such as on certain soils shortly after a rain. Observe the different types of soils and trail construction and practice minimum impact cycling. This also means staying on the trail and not creating new ones. Be sure to pack out at least as much as you pack into an area.

3. **CONTROL YOUR BICYCLE!** Inattention for even a second can mean disaster for yourself or others. Excessive speed threatens people. There is no excuse for it!

4. **ALWAYS YIELD THE TRAIL.** Make known your approach well in advance. A friendly greeting (or bell) is considerate and works well. Show your respect when passing others by slowing to a walk or stopping all together. Anticipate that other trail users may be around corners or in blind spots.

5. **PUT SOMETHING BACK.** I have spent enough time building and maintaining trails to tell you it is every bit as rewarding as an epic trip. If everyone put just a fraction of their riding time back into the trails, we could ensure great places to ride well into the future. It is all of our responsibility.

Table of Contents

East Tennessee, Cont.

Middle Tennessee

West Tennessee

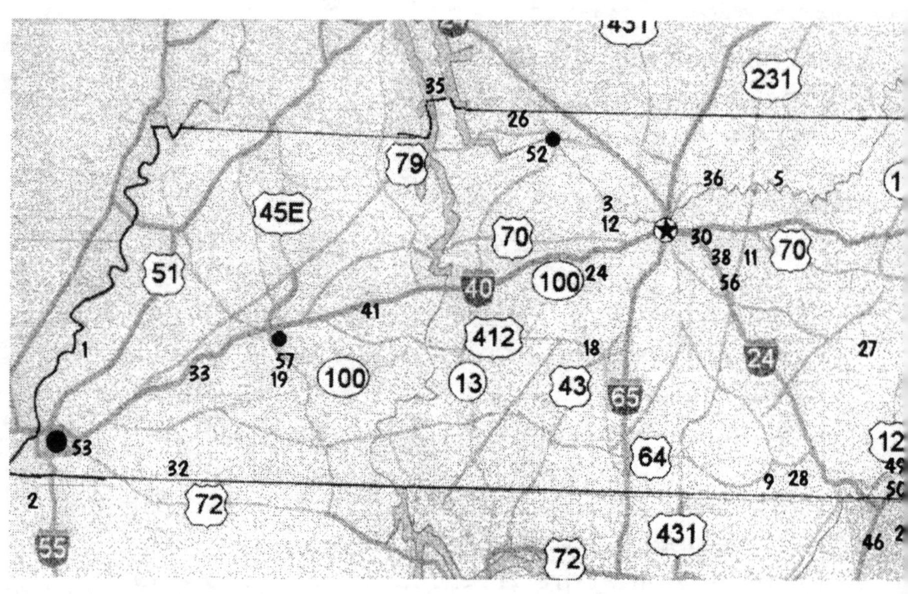

Anderson Tully	1
Arkabutla Lake	2
Ashland City RR	3
Bear Creek, GA	4
Bearwaller Gap	5
Big South Fork	6
Black Mountain	7
Cades Cove	8
Carter WMA	9
Catoosa WMA	10
Cedars of Lebanon	11
Cheatham WMA	12
Cherokee Nat'l Forest	
Hiwasee	13
Nolichucky	14
Ocoee	15
Unaka	16
Wautuga	17
Chickasaw S.F.	18
Chickasaw N.W.R.	19
Chuck Swan	20
Conasaunga River	21
Eastern State	22
Edward's Point	23
Fairview	24
Five Points, GA	25
Fort Campbell ORV	26
Fall Creek Falls	27
Franklin S.F.	28
Green River SP	29
Hamilton Creek	30
Haw Ridge	31

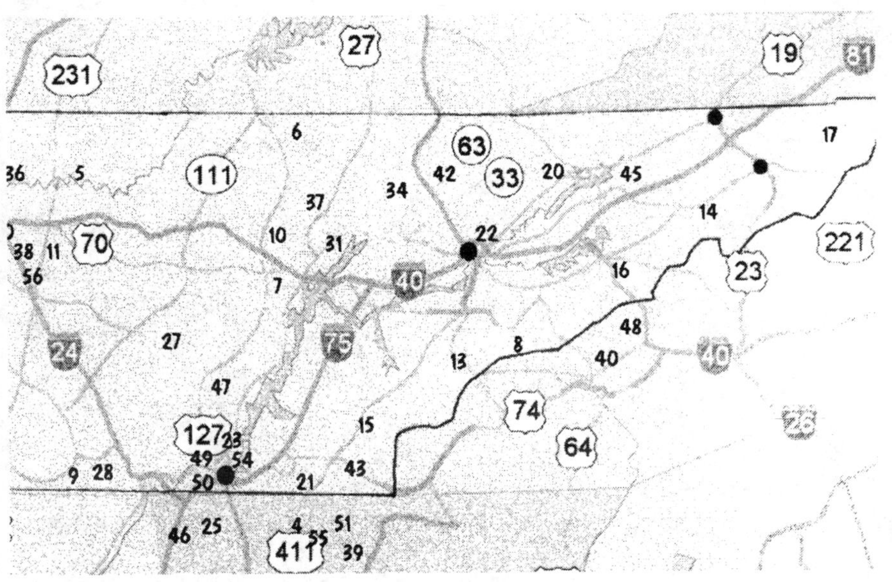

Herb Parsons S.P.	32	Panther Creek	45
Hatchie N.W.F.	33	Pigeon Mountain	46
Indian Bluff	34	Piney River	47
L.B.L.	35	Pisgah	48
Lock 4	36	Prentice Cooper	49
Lone Mountain	37	Raccoon Mountain	50
Long Hunter SP	38	Rich Mountain	51
M.O.E.	39	Rotary Park	52
Nantahala/Tsali	40	Shelby Farms	53
Natchez Trace S.P	41	Stringers Ridge	54
Norris	42	Tatem Lead	55
Ocoee		Twin Forks	56
Chilhowee Mtn	43	Youth Town	57
Conasauga River	44		

DAM AREA AND HERNANDO POINT

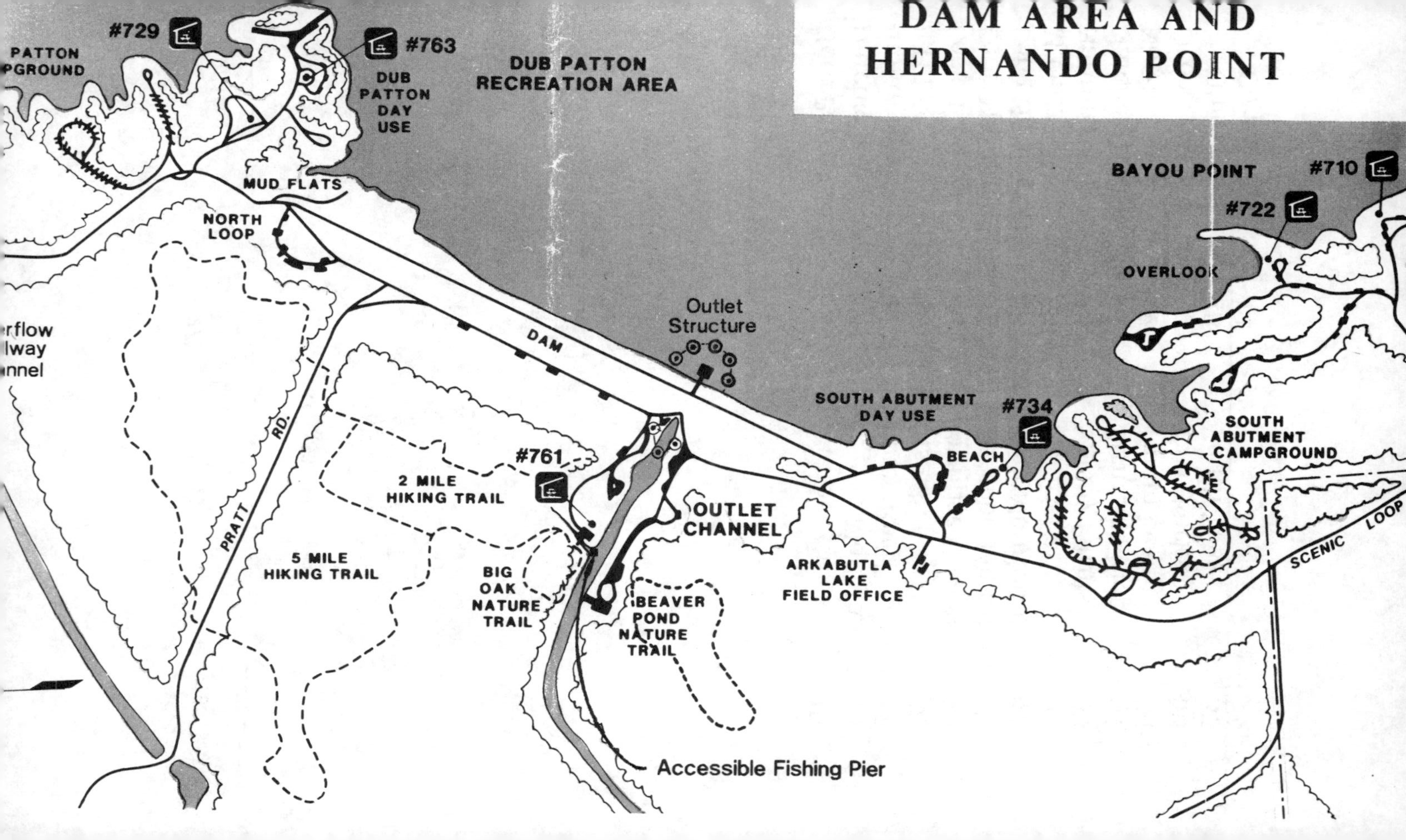

ARKABUTLA LAKE

Arkabutla Lake is the U.S. Army Corps of Engineers project closest to Memphis. It receives nearly 2 million visitors each year and has become a popular mountain biking area, hosting several races and events recently.

There is one main hiking trail to ride on. It is a five-mile loop that leaves from picnic area 761. With a two-mile trail and Pratt Road connecting the trail, you can create several different loops. After you finish riding you can go to the beach for a swim or play volleyball.

Directions: From Memphis take I-55 south to Hernando, 304 West to Eudora, MS. Then turn south on 301 to Pratt Road. (301 dead ends onto Pratt Rd.) Turn left and follow the signs into the park.

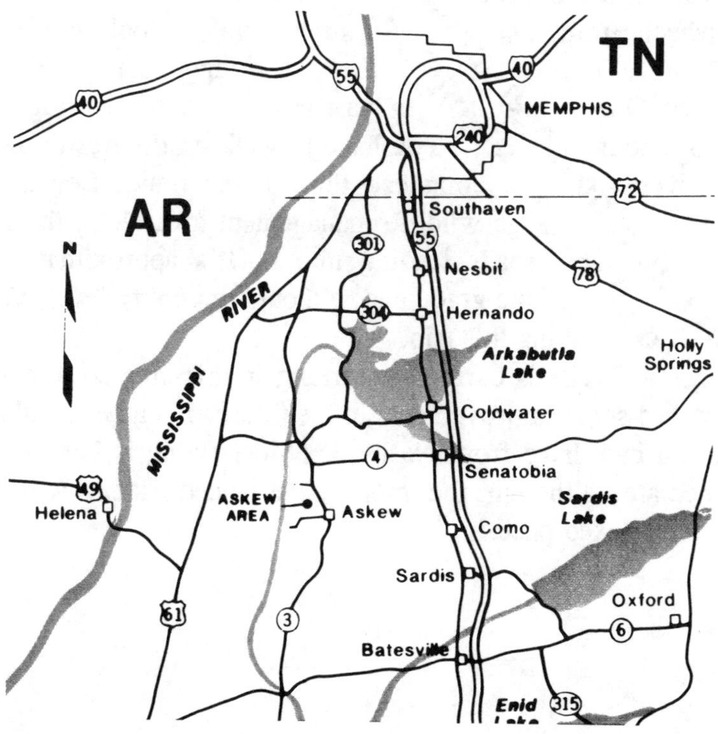

ASHLAND CITY RR

This trail is no longer maintained and many of the sections have closed all access. Riding is no longer advised here. 5/96

This is a great place to bring the family to ride. [illegible] along the Cumberland River, the grade is protected o[illegible] by trees and on the other by towering bluffs. The t[illegible] about 15 miles. The parking area is located close t[illegible] so depending on which direction you take you can [illegible] 20-mile trip (out and back).

If you ride north, you'll pass a numbe[illegible] ponds and lodges. It is rumored the large mound [illegible]ver is an old Indian burial ground. You'll encounte[illegible]ep banks where the bridges have been removed. T[illegible]ryone a chance to test their hill-climbing skills. I'[illegible]en past the creek at the north end of this trail, b[illegible]nd the grade continues on. There are also some si[illegible]e adventurous.

Heading south from [illegible] lot, the grade is more of a four-wheeler trail. Th[illegible]imb to an overlook on the left. You'll have to sk[illegible] the old bridges that have been removed. One a[illegible]er here is an abandoned bridge that runs for about [illegible] You have to walk on the trestle over a small river [illegible]commend this for the timid. Beyond the bridge, t[illegible]ge wildlife management area along the river with s[illegible] roads leading into it. It's approximately 10 mile[illegible] of the grade and, although its pretty level, you'll b[illegible] making this trip.

[illegible] Trails is currently working in this area so hopefully [illegible] see some improvements in the future. It's a beautiful area an[illegible] not a bad drive from Nashville. Most riding is beginner or intermediate, although the more experienced riders will also enjoy the relaxed pace.

Directions: From Nashville take I-24 west to exit 24. Follow Rt. 49 west toward Ashland City, approximately five miles. Turn right on Sweethome Rd. and follow it for six or seven miles. At the stop sign, go straight across until you reach the river. To find the grade (it's not advertised), park in the first parking area you come to. The grade runs along the trees against the bluff. You'll see a dirt road going left and right as you get closer.

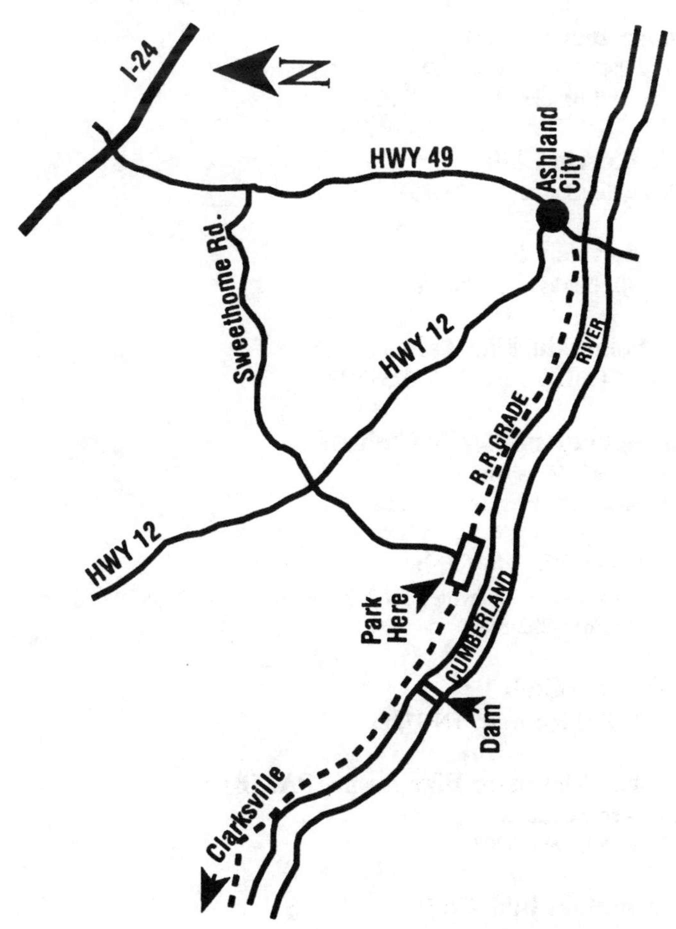

Mountain Bike Clubs

Appalachian Mountain Bike Club
PO Box 53384, Knoxville, TN 37950-3384
Paul Wolf 423-281-0195

Bicycle Federation of Tennessee
PO Box 2823, Murfreesboro, TN 37130

Big South Fork Bicycle Club
PO Box 4129, Oneida, TN 37841
Joe Cross, 423-569-9186, 569-8652

Chattanooga Bicycle Club
PO Box 21843, Chattanooga, TN 37421-0843
President, Bill Brooks, 423-344-0710

Cookeville Bicycle Club
123 Moore St., Sparta, TN 38583

Kennessee Bicycle Club
PO Box 140, Clarksville, TN 37041

Kentucky Mountain Bike Assn.,
P.O. Box 5344, Louisville, KY 40255-0433

Memphis Hightailers Bicycle Club
PO Box 111195, Memphis, TN 38111
VP Off Road, Tom Ferguson 901-853-7272

Mountain Trails Bicycle Club
3617 Westbrook Ave, Nashville, TN 37205
Stephen Carr, 615-292-8691

Nashville Bicycle Club
PO Box 158593, Nashville, TN 37215

Purchase Area Mountain Bike Assn. (PAMBA)
Land Between the Lakes
Chad Cash, (502) 898-3207

Sewanee Mountain Bike Club
PO Box 822, Sewanee, TN 37375

BLACK MOUNTAIN

This is a little known area that is home to section 5 of the Cumberland Trail and nearly 100 miles of four-wheeler and jeep roads. Most is uncharted and you will not find many maps of the trails. The land is owned in part by the United Methodist Church and Cumberland Cove. It is rugged, vast and there is open access with an endless selection of jeep roads to explore.

The terrain is quite extreme, rocky with lots of long descents and climbs. There are several ways to access the riding. You can park on top of the mountain; the Cumberland Trail heads off behind the tower on top. The rock formations are out of this world, a rock climber's paradise. The Cumberland Trail is blazed in white and heads straight down the mountain to Grassy Cove. If it is all in tact, there's a 20-mile trail covering two mountain ranges. The state no longer maintains this area, however, four-wheelers most likely have kept it open. The last I heard, the trail was accessible to the summit of Brady Mountain.

We parked at Owl Gap Roost, the first main jeep road on the left as you head up the mountain. It is a well worn and you can't miss it. After appx. two miles you will come to a four-way junction. Straight leads along the top through an old clear-cut. Left heads downhill on a smaller four-wheeler trail through a drainage and connects with another trail after a mile. Another left is a long uphill that circles back to the car. Right is a fast downhill leading to a network of singletrack trails at the bottom.

We weren't able to explore as far as we wanted but whoever is building the trails has done a great job. They are packed by the motorcycles and are well marked. There is supposed to be a singletrack network along the mountain. I will be back to explore it all.

You can also park at the bottom of the mountain closer to the interstate. You could park one car and end your ride at the bottom, if you can find your way.

Directions: Black Mountain is just outside of Crab Orchard, TN, east of Crossville. Exit there and go over the interstate and follow this curvy road for 1.5 miles to the crossroads. Turn left, and head up, up, up. You can park at the jeep road at Owl Roost Gap, or continue another mile to the top of Black Mountain.

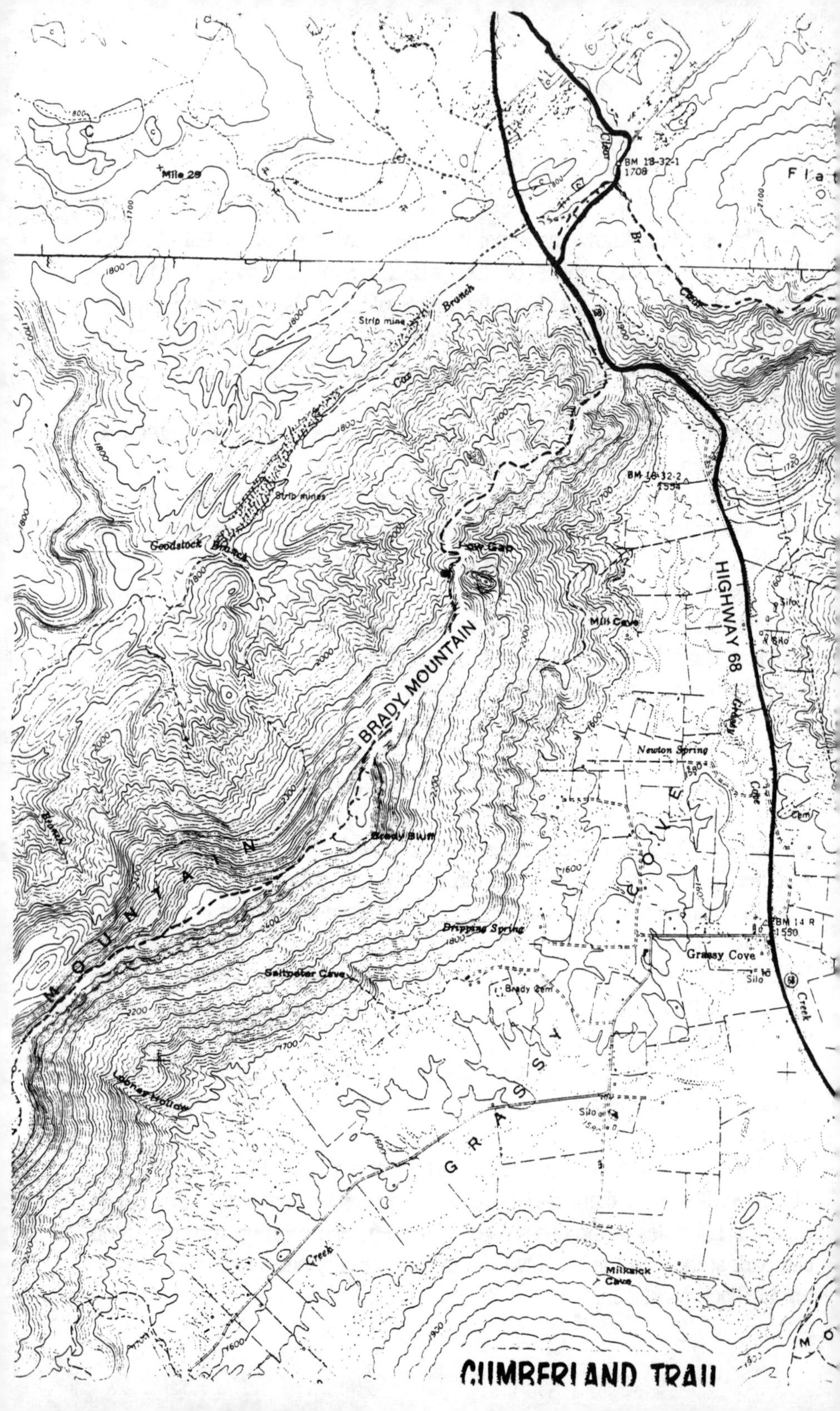

Mile 29
BM 18-32-1
1708
Flat
Strip mine
Branch
Strip mines
Goodstock Branch
Low Gap
BM 18-32-2
1554
HIGHWAY 68
Mill Cave
BRADY MOUNTAIN
Newton Spring
Silo
Brady BWM
COVE
MOUNTAIN
Dripping Spring
BM 14 R
1550
Grassy Cove
Saltpeter Cave
Brady Cem
GRASSY
Looney Hollow
Creek
Milksick
Cave
CUMBERLAND TRAIL

STATES
F THE INTERIOR
AL SURVEY
BLACK MOUNTAIN
Black Mountain
Owl Roost Gap
Haley Mtn
The Basin
Cove
Hollow
DUG HILL RIDGE
Little Cove
Bristow Sem
Ruins
PRIVATE
Loden Mountain
Loden Ridge
Loden Branch
Stillhouse Hollow
Harris Branch
Partridge Spring
Strip mine
South Fork
North
Shinbone

BEAR CREEK, GA.

Located just an hour south of Chattanooga and east of Dalton are the mountains of northern Georgia. With the help of SORBA, mountain bikers are allowed to ride in many of Georgia's state parks. There are many miles of single track hiking trails and fire roads. You'll find lots of challenging climbs, hair-raising down hills that go on for miles, and some of the most beautiful scenery south of the Smokies. Park rangers are happy to talk to you about the trails, some of which are suitable to all rider levels. However a lot of the off-road riding is rough, rocky, steep, and technical. Aggressive riders will love everything about this place.

Popular rides include the **Bear Creek** trail, an approximately 10-mile ride that is rated for beginners and intermediate riders. From the Bear Creek campground, ride back to the Forest Service Road and begin the four-mile climb. It's not bad, just continuous. Barnes Creek Falls is a good rest stop. Further up, the trail goes right at the gate. This is the Barnes Creek ORV trail. I suggest you go another 500 yards up the Forest Service Road for a spectacular overlook.

Several hundred yards past the gate on Barnes Creek, take the branch that goes right. At the bottom of the hill go right through the gate and down the next hill. When you enter a small clearing, the trail will make a very sharp left turn. (You'll have to look for it.) Go over two big humps, and the fun continues all the way down the mountain. There is another sharp right-hand switch back, then follow the creek home. You can also take the trail leading left for a longer loop. Plan on spending 1 1/2 to 2 hours on this trip. This was the course for the '90 and '91 Georgia State Championships.

If you don't need electricity and running water, the Bear Creek Campground is a cool place to camp and ride from. Otherwise you can camp at the Fort Payne State Campground. They have hot showers, electricity, a lake and plenty of bears.

If you're feeling really ambitious, **Mountaintown Creek** is a more advanced 24-mile loop. You ride up the Bear Creek trail along the creek and ride to the 180-degree overlook. Continue up the mountain for another 1.5 miles until you reach a T junction of FS 68 and FS 64 (Potato Patch Mtn.). Turn right and ride along FS 68 several miles to the Three Forks Mtn. parking area, then downhill for 2.5 miles until you see the brown sign for Mountaintown Creek trail (Orange Blaze). This is what you worked for. From here you'll have seven miles of singletrack that's all downhill. The little stream on your left is Mountaintown Creek. As it grows there will be waterfalls, lots of rapids, and a much larger creek to cross. The trail levels out as you near the parking area. Follow the dirt road all the way out. Don't take any turnoffs. Once you reach pavement go right. This will take you back to the campground. Plan on spending four hours to complete this ride, and bring lots of food and water.

Windy Gap is another popular ride when visiting the Cohutta WMA. It offers some of the most challenging and extreme riding in the area. You can start in two locations. The Lake Conasauge campground is up on top, and you can start with some expert only singletrack straight down the mountain. Then turn left on Milma and follow it to Tibbs Creek. Take the *first hard left* on Tibbs and climb straight back up the mountain to the campground. It's an awesome, expert ride. You can also park on the main road 4.3 miles east of Eton, ride up Tibbs (gravel) to Milma, follow it to Windy Gap and downhill all the way back to your car. The Climb up Tibbs seems non-ending but is another great loop for mountain riding. The bottom of Windy Gap is getting pretty washed out, caution is recommended.

Directions; From Chatsworth, take US 52 east about 17 miles. You will drive past the Fort Mountain S.P., then past a motel on the right. Look for Tatum Lead trailhead on your right. Continue on for several more miles. Turn left on Gates Chapel Rd. there is a directional sign on Hwy. 52 hidden in a corner. You will reach the turn-off to Bear Creek in 4.6 miles. Turn right on the Gravel Bear Creek Road, FS 241 for two miles to the campground. This is excellent primitive camping. Fort Mountain S.P. offers showers, etc.. For more information, contact the Cohutta Ranger District, 706-695-6736.

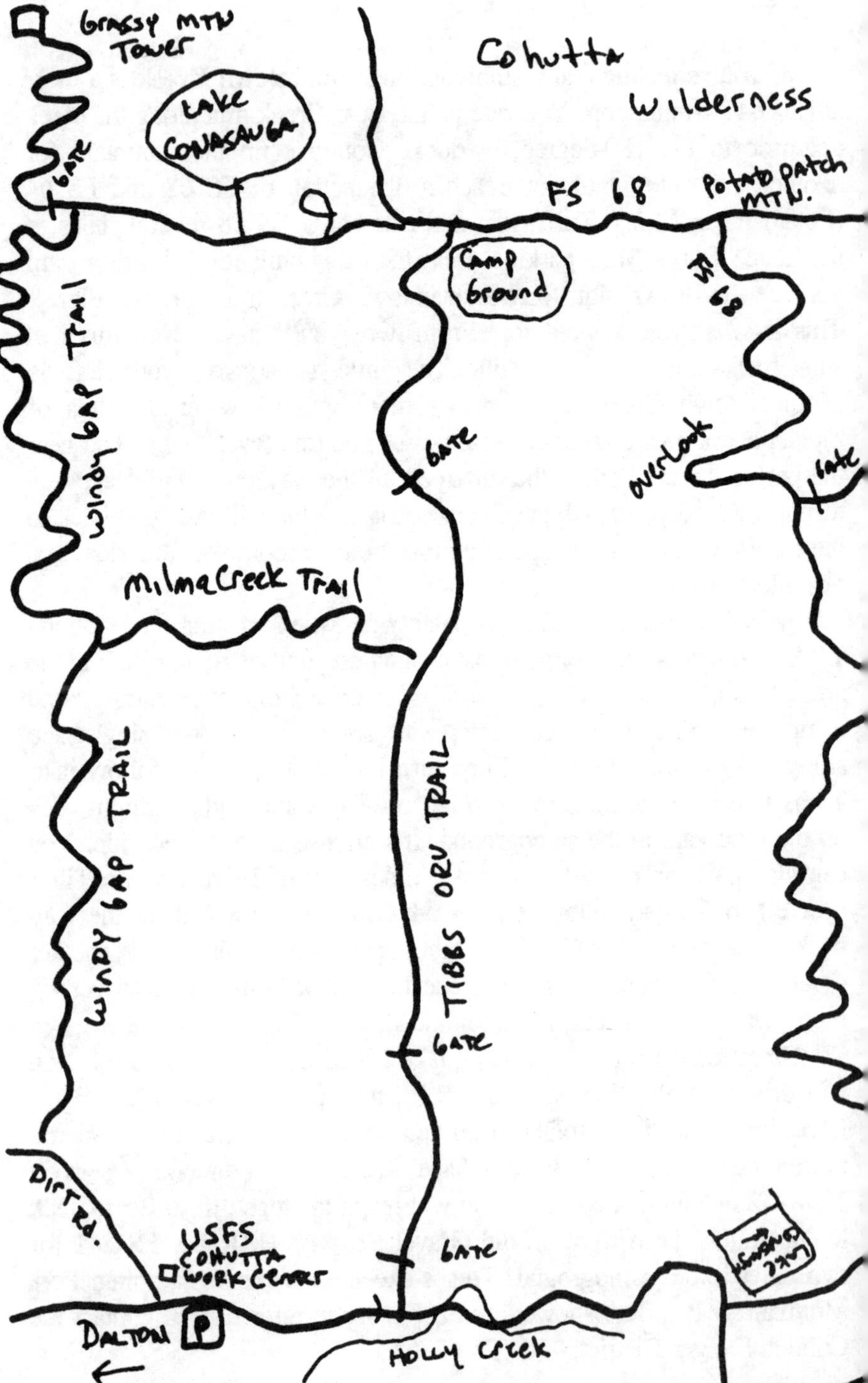

Grassy Mtn Tower

Lake Conasauga

Cohutta Wilderness

Gate

FS 68

Potato patch Mtn.

Camp ground

FS 68

Windy Gap Trail

Gate

overlook

Gate

Milma Creek Trail

Windy Gap Trail

Tibbs ORV Trail

Gate

Dirt Rd.

USFS Cohutta Work Center

Gate

Dalton

P

Holly Creek

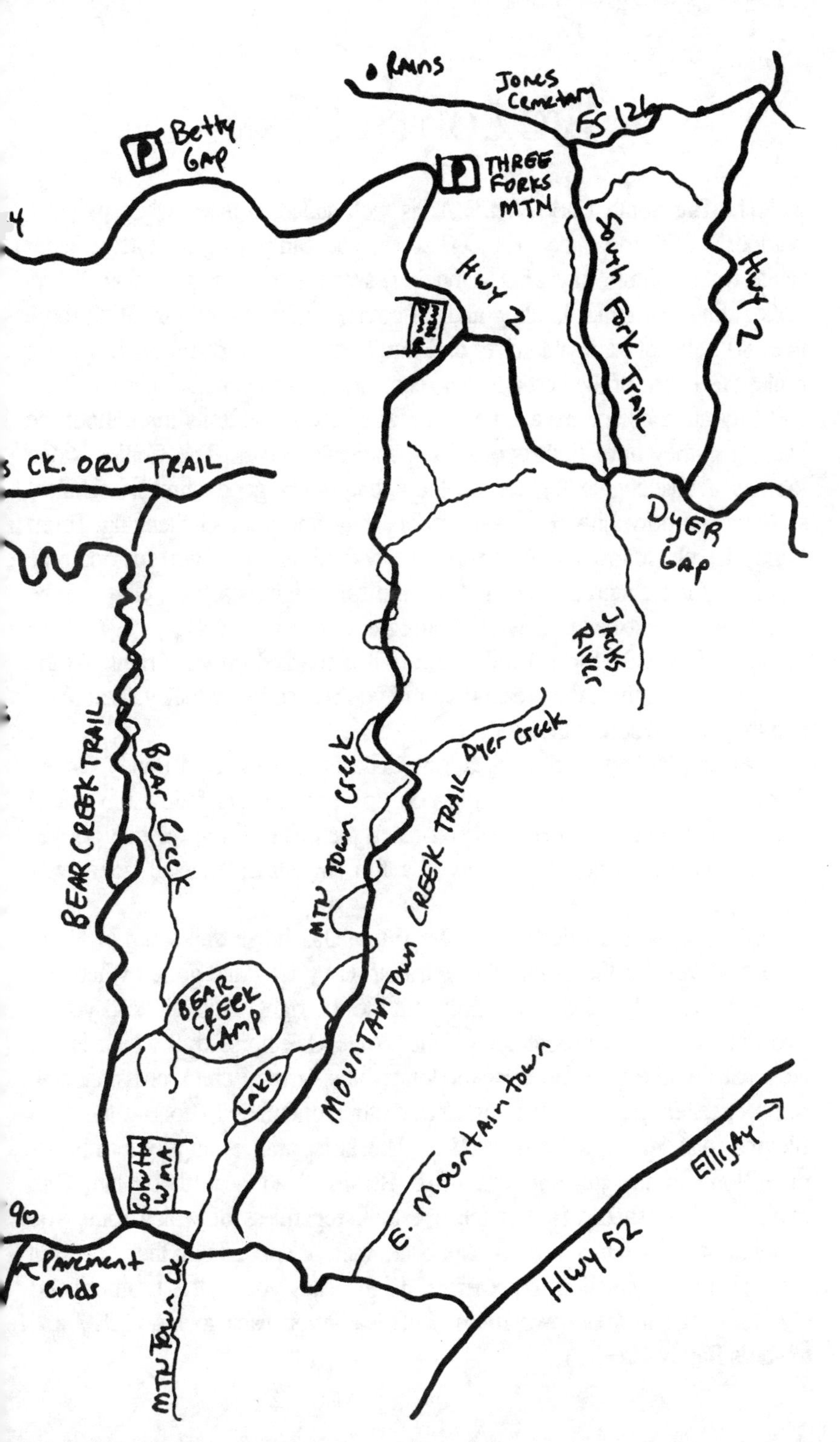

o Rains
Jones Cemetary
FS 12
P
Betty Gap
P
THREE FORKS MTN
4
Hwy 2
South Fork Trail
Hwy 2
s CK. ORV TRAIL
Dyer Gap
Jacks River
Dyer creek
BEAR CREEK TRAIL
Bear Creek
MTN Town Creek
MOUNTAINTOWN CREEK TRAIL
BEAR CREEK CAMP
LAKE
E. Mountaintown
Ellijay →
Cohutta WMA
90
Hwy 52
← Pavement ends
MTN Town Ck

BIG SOUTH FORK

The Big South Fork N.R.R.A. is well suited to those who enjoy the outdoors. With more than 100,000 acres, you can pursue such activities as white water rafting, kayaking, canoeing, swimming, fishing, hiking, horseback riding, camping, hunting and, of course, mountain biking. With more than 80 miles of navigable river and hundreds of miles of hiking and horse trails, this is one of the best outdoor recreation areas Tennessee has to offer.

Mountain bikers are allowed on any of the horse trails throughout the park, and they have built two trails specifically for us. The Collier Ridge loop is a challenging eight mile loop that offers good climbs, technical sections and downhills. Beginning riders may find it too challenging. From Bandy Creek, follow the main road (the pool is on your right) for one mile and look for the sign on your left. At the split, right is a good climb to the top, (it's a much better downhill) straight comes out on Hwy. 297. Turn right on Hwy. 297 for 1.3 miles, the trail is marked on your right. At the next junction, right is the great down hill you passed in the valley. Left leads to a longer loop across the road.

Duncan Hollow is 5.3 miles long and also leaves from Bandy Creek. Take the road with the swimming pool to your left and follow the gravel road with the cycle markers. As you reach the power lines, the trail goes to the left and heads downhill. This is a fun singletrack trail all riders will enjoy.

Other suggested rides include the White Oak horse trail south of Hwy. 297. You can ride the Collier Ridge trail to Hwy. 287 and go left when you reach the road, then follow the horse trail to the right. This will lead you to two options. You can continue on the White Oak horse trail which is my personal favorite ride. It offers moderate hills, several creek crossings and some excellent singletrack trails. Your other option is to follow the Gap Blevins road left when you reach it. The horse trail is approximately six miles long to the junction with Gap Blevins road near the White Oak overlook. You should ride to the overlook regardless of which route you choose. On your return trip you can back track or continue on the horse trail east. There is a junction in six miles. Right leads you to the Leatherwood Overlook trail in about two miles. Left leads you back to Hwy. 297 and towards Bandy Creek.

If you want a scenic, easy ride, the O&W railroad grade follows the White Oak Creek offering a relaxing ride with outstanding scenery. To access the parking area, drive west of the park and follow Toomay Road south to the parking area near some oil wells. From that point, it is a nice ride down to the O&W bridge. This is a "must see" for all. You'll ride below towering bluffs, and the bridge over the river is spectacular. During the spring, you'll be entertained by river runners. To ride the railroad grade along White Oak Creek, there is one river crossing where you will get wet. Once you're across, it's easy riding along the fast flowing creek. This is an excellent trip to take your family on. You can also access the grade from Gernt Road or the Coyle Branch Trail. I only recommend these routes for advanced riders.

If you are a true adventurer, ask one of the rangers about a trip from Bandy Creek up to Terry's Cemetery. Then drop down into No Business Creek, (it was better before the gravel). Next is the huge climb out, when you reach splitrock, you're halfway up Peter's Mountain. We have done this a couple of times, it is an incredible day. I suggest parking a car or having someone pick you up on top of Peter's Mountain. It is a good place to end your ride. Ask about trail conditions, the horses have had a negative impact on many of these trails and they could now be unrideable.

The Big South Fork is a great place to bring your family. There's so much to see and do. If you have time, take a hike along the John Muhr trail. You'll walk along bluffs hundreds of feet above the river. If you prefer, do a little fishing, rent some horses, or just lay by the pool. There are several outfitters who offer rock climbing, rafting, and canoe trips. The Big South Fork is famous for its white water; take your group through the gorge for a trip that won't soon be forgotten.

Camping is allowed anywhere in the park. There are campgrounds at Bandy Creek with hot showers and electricity available. You'll also find several hotels nearby. I've not tried it yet, but the Chariot Creek Hostel is supposed to be a great place to spend the night.

For more information: Big South Fork N.R.R.A., Rt. 3, Box 401, Oneida, TN 37841, 423-879-3625. The rangers will be happy to talk with you about trails suitable for all abilities. Maps can be purchased in the office. Outfitters are also available to rent all types of equipment.

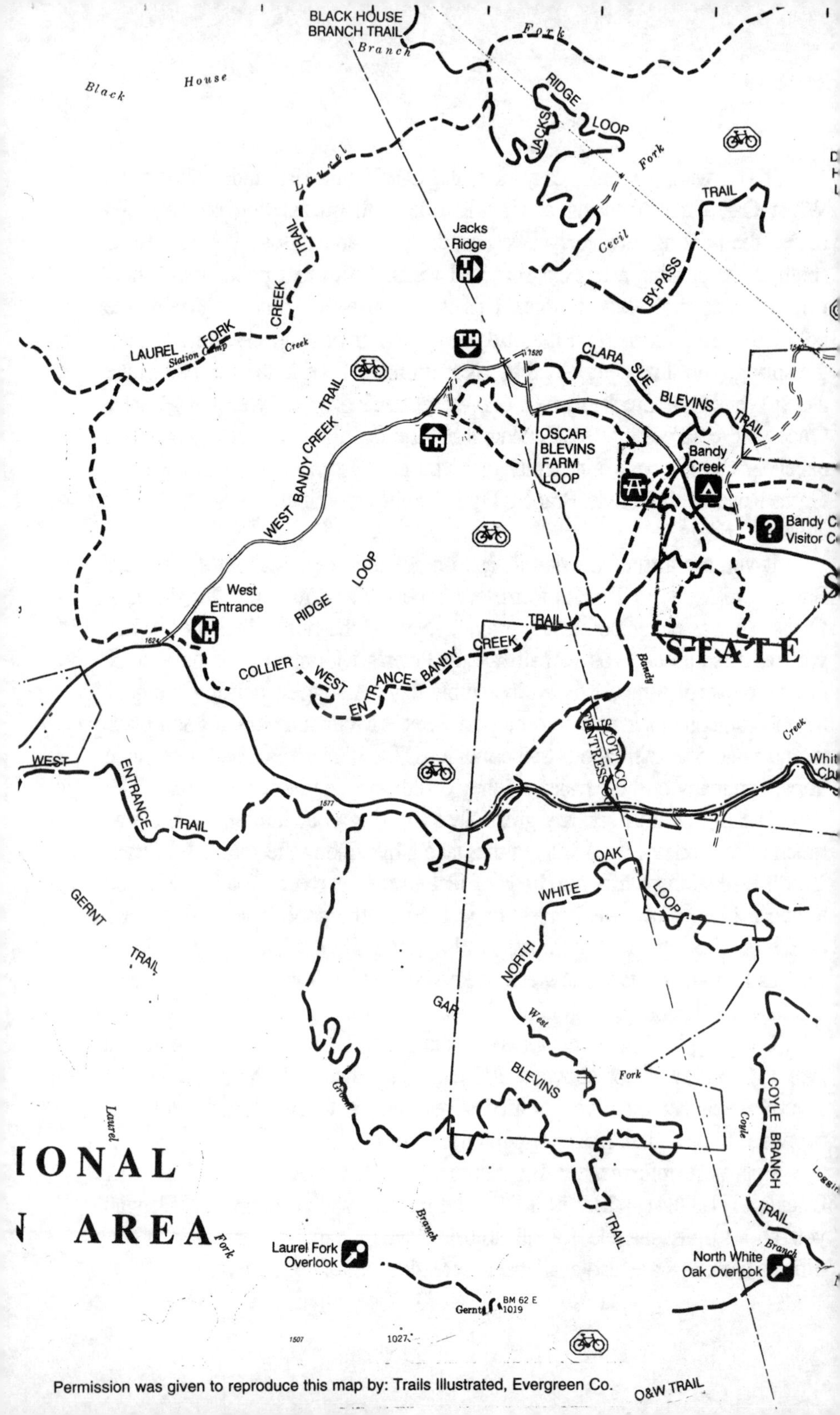

Permission was given to reproduce this map by: Trails Illustrated, Evergreen Co.

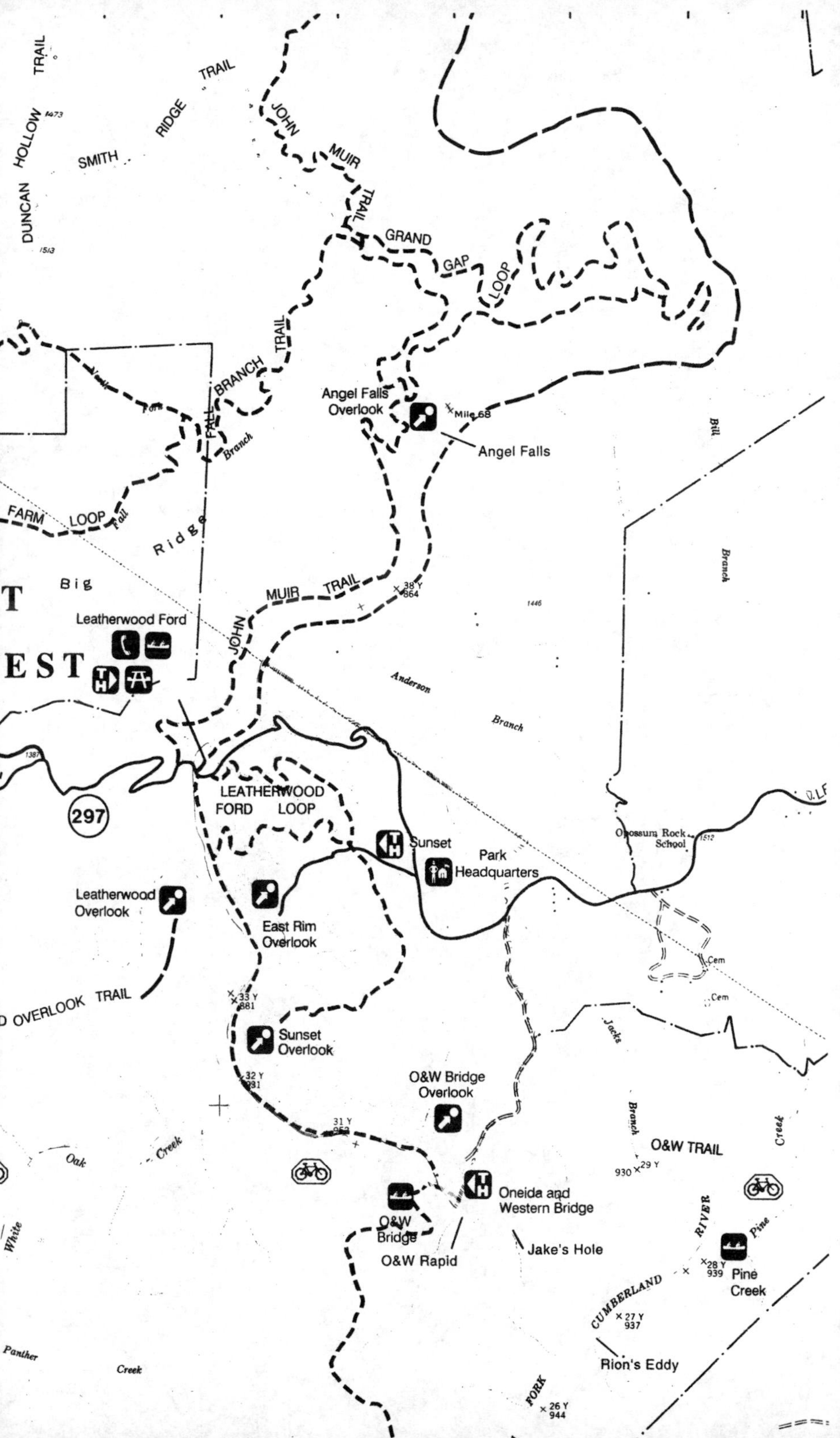

DUNCAN HOLLOW TRAIL
SMITH RIDGE TRAIL
JOHN MUIR TRAIL
GRAND GAP LOOP
FALL BRANCH TRAIL
Angel Falls Overlook
Mile 68
Angel Falls
FARM LOOP
Ridge
Big
Leatherwood Ford
JOHN MUIR TRAIL
38 Y 864
Anderson Branch
Bill Branch
1446
LEATHERWOOD FORD LOOP
297
Sunset
Park Headquarters
Opossum Rock School
Leatherwood Overlook
East Rim Overlook
OVERLOOK TRAIL
33 Y 881
Sunset Overlook
Cem
Jacks Branch
32 Y 931
O&W Bridge Overlook
31 Y 953
Oak Creek
O&W TRAIL
930 29 Y
Oneida and Western Bridge
O&W Bridge
O&W Rapid
Jake's Hole
RIVER
Pine
28 Y 939
Pine Creek
CUMBERLAND
27 Y 937
Rion's Eddy
FORK
26 Y 944
White
Panther
Creek

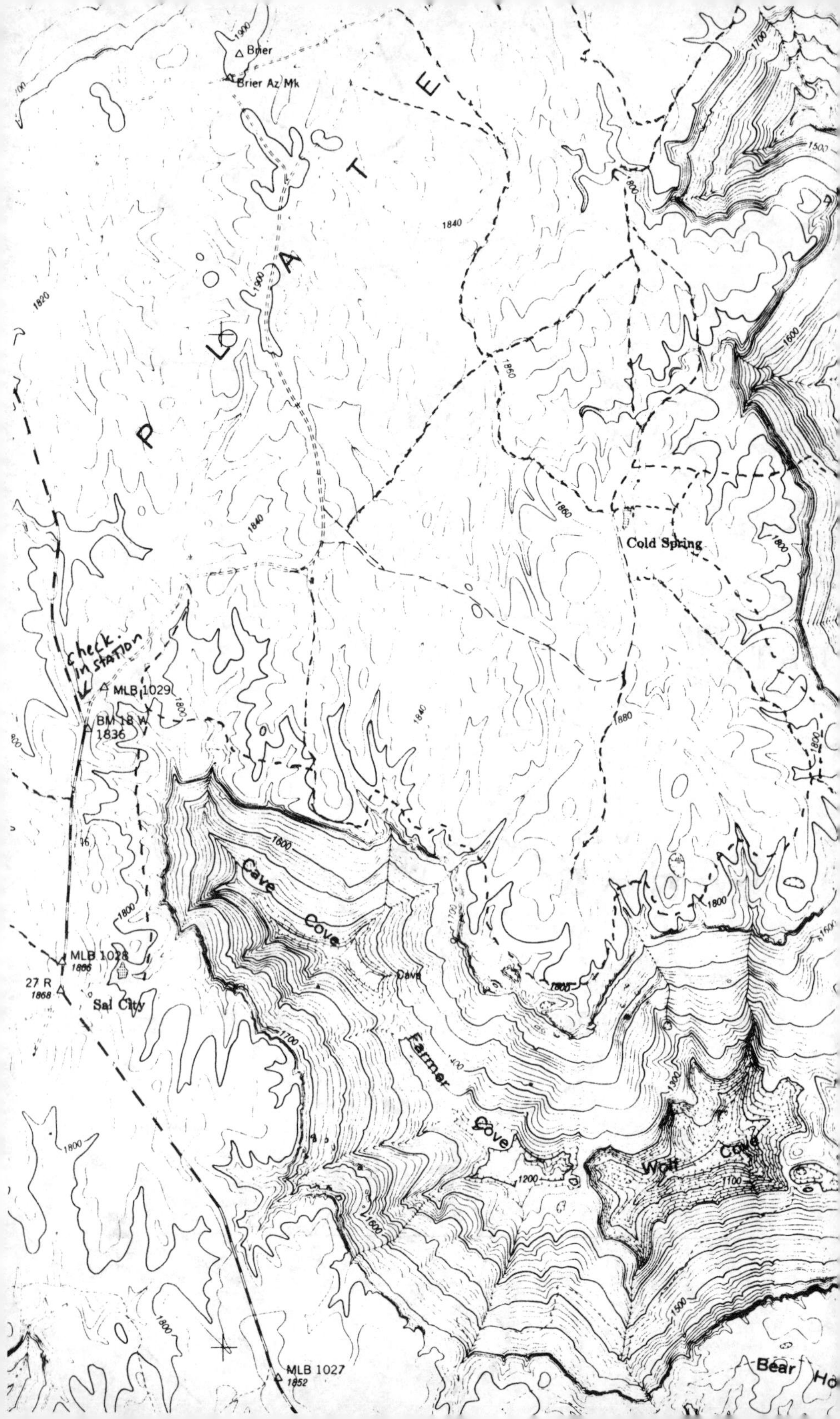

Brier
Brier Az Mk
P L A T E
Check in station
MLB 1029
BM 18 W
1836
MLB 1028
1866
27 R
1868
Sal City
Cave Cove
Cave
Farmer Cove
Wolf Cove
Cold Spring
MLB 1027
1852
Bear
1840
1860
1880
1820
1800
1900
1700
1600
1500
1200
1100

Carter W.M.A.

This is another large tract of land that offers unlimited riding on any type of terrain. Hunters and four-wheelers have created a network of trails that run along the rim. For the most part the trail is rolling without any major climbs. If you're looking for a more adventurous trip you can turn left and find 700' - 800' vertical descents dropping off the ridge. Remember, you must climb back up to your car and these trails are not marked.

Depending on what you prefer to ride on, the main road is gravel. From there, you'll find jeep and four-wheeler trails that go on for miles. I suggest a fun single track trail that leads from Cold Water Spring along the bluffs of Cave and Farmer Coves. This is fairly technical with moderate elevation changes. Starting at the check-in station, it's a 10-mile loop. If you feel adventurous, try a side road.

Directions: Located just 13 miles from Winchester, take Hwy. 64 W 1.4 miles to Hwy. 16 south. It's 6.4 miles to the deer check-in station. You can park here or drive down the gravel road to Cold Spring. There are trails in every direction from here. The single track is a little tricky to find—just keep following the trail that runs along the back side of the pond. Bring your own water and supplies as none are available here. Camping is allowed, although it is primitive.

This map is just a small portion of the riding that's available. Topo maps are available and feature endless jeep roads. I suggest bringing one to do some exploring.

Chuck Swan W.M.A.

Located between Tazwell and LaFollette, Chuck Swan offers 25,000 acres of rolling hills surrounded by Norris Lake. Gravel roads provide access to most of the area, while logging roads travel throughout. I spoke with Manager Phil Bledsoe, who told me only hikers and mountain bikers were allowed on the logging roads. He realizes we are low-impact users.

This is another beautiful area to visit, with more than 100 miles of lake frontage, 4,000 deer and plenty of other wildlife to see. Bring your family, ride down to the lake and have a picnic.

Directions: There is only one way into Chuck Swan. Take Hwy. 33 north from Knoxville. Once you cross over the Clinch River, take the first left (Sharpe Chapel Rd.). Follow it to Main Forest Rd., which leads you to the Checking Station. For more information, call Phil Bledsoe, 423-278-3248.

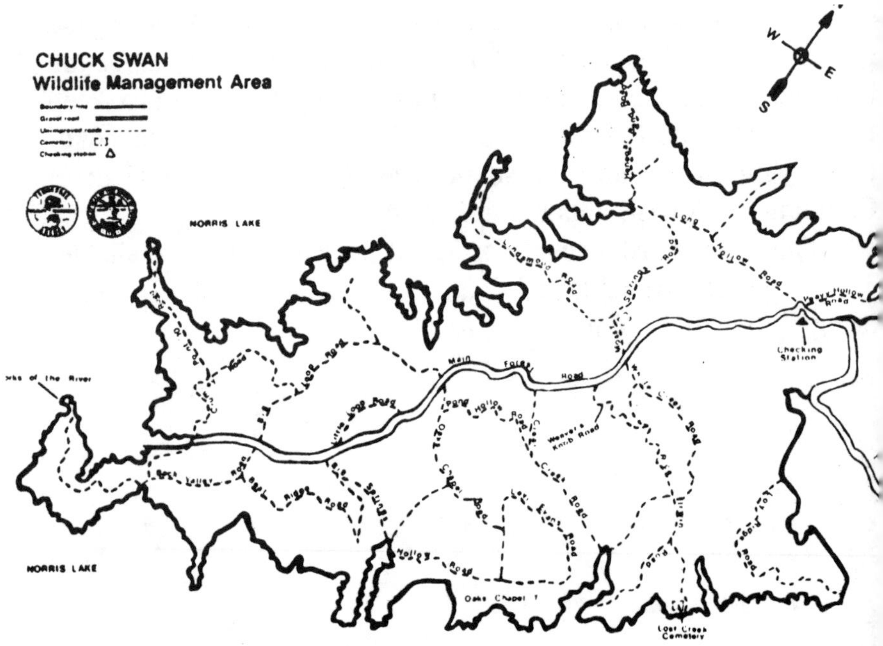

CATOOSA WILDLIFE MGMT. AREA

The Catoosa Wildlife Management Area is the largest tract of land administered and owned by the Tennessee Wildlife Resources Agency. Consisting of approximately 80,000 acres in Cumberland, Morgan, and Fentress counties, this vast region is located 20 miles north of Crossville and stretches east across the Cumberland Plateau and into the Cumberland Mountains near Wartburg. Running within Catoosa are a number of very popular white water rivers including the Obed, Daddy's, Clear and Otter Creeks.

Elevations on the Catoosa range from 1,100 feet to more than 2,300 feet. These are the hills of the Cumberland Plateau, and they provide a variety of excellent mountain biking. Currently, there are 70 miles of gravel roads, 40 miles of large stone roads and 150 miles of trails. We have ridden near Otter and Daddy's Creek recently and can't believe the possibilities. Trail conditions vary from four-wheeler to gravel jeep roads, and all were in good condition. The riding west of Daddy's creek is less challenging elevation wise and we found several nice 10 - 15 mile loops, with plenty of side trips.

Once you cross the gorge the riding becomes much steeper and more technical. There is a great trail that leads from the Pilot Knob Firetower all along Hatfield Mountain. It is an out and back but extends for more than 8 miles. A wild side trip drops off Hatfield Ridge after 2.7 miles into Turkey Creek. This is a hair-raising technical ride down a drainage and back up the other side. See the map for details.

I would like to remind everyone that Tennessee's W.M.A.'s are paid for by hunters and fishermen. We are not allowed to be there during big game or turkey season. Catoosa closes it's gates to everyone from February 1 - March 31 each year for the wildlife to breed.

For more information: Catoosa WMA 423-456-2479, or the Obed River Ranger Station, Wartburg, 423-346-6295. The rangers in Wartburg will be happy to steer you to some great trails. There is an excellent 4' x 6' topo map available. Call MJC Maps 800-213-6147.

Directions: Most of the easier riding is accessed off Peavine Road. Take exit 322 off I-40. Go north 1.7 miles and turn left on Firetower Rd. You will enter the park in 3 miles. The first small gorge is Otter Creek, 5 miles later you hit Daddy's Creek. To reach the firetower, follow Peavine Rd. through Daddy's Ck. Turn left on Nemo Rd. and park at the intersection. Ride the road to the left and the trail goes right at the gate.

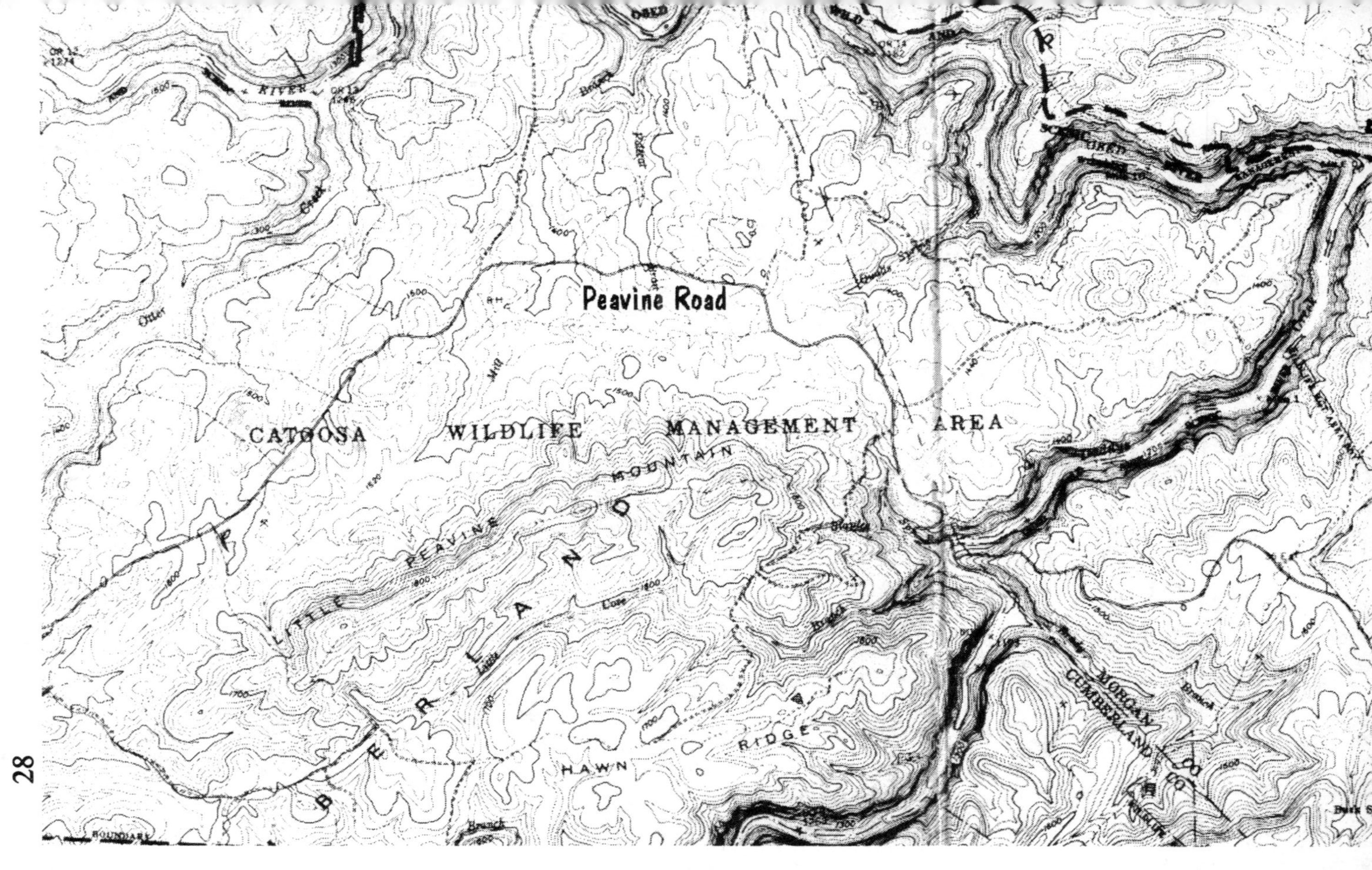

Peavine Road
CATOOSA WILDLIFE MANAGEMENT AREA
LITTLE PEAVINE MOUNTAIN
HAWN RIDGE
MORGAN CO
CUMBERLAND CO

Peavine Rd.
M O U N T A I N
Nemo Rd.
Pilot Knob
Pilot Knob Mountain
H A T F I E L D
M O U N T A I N
To Nemo

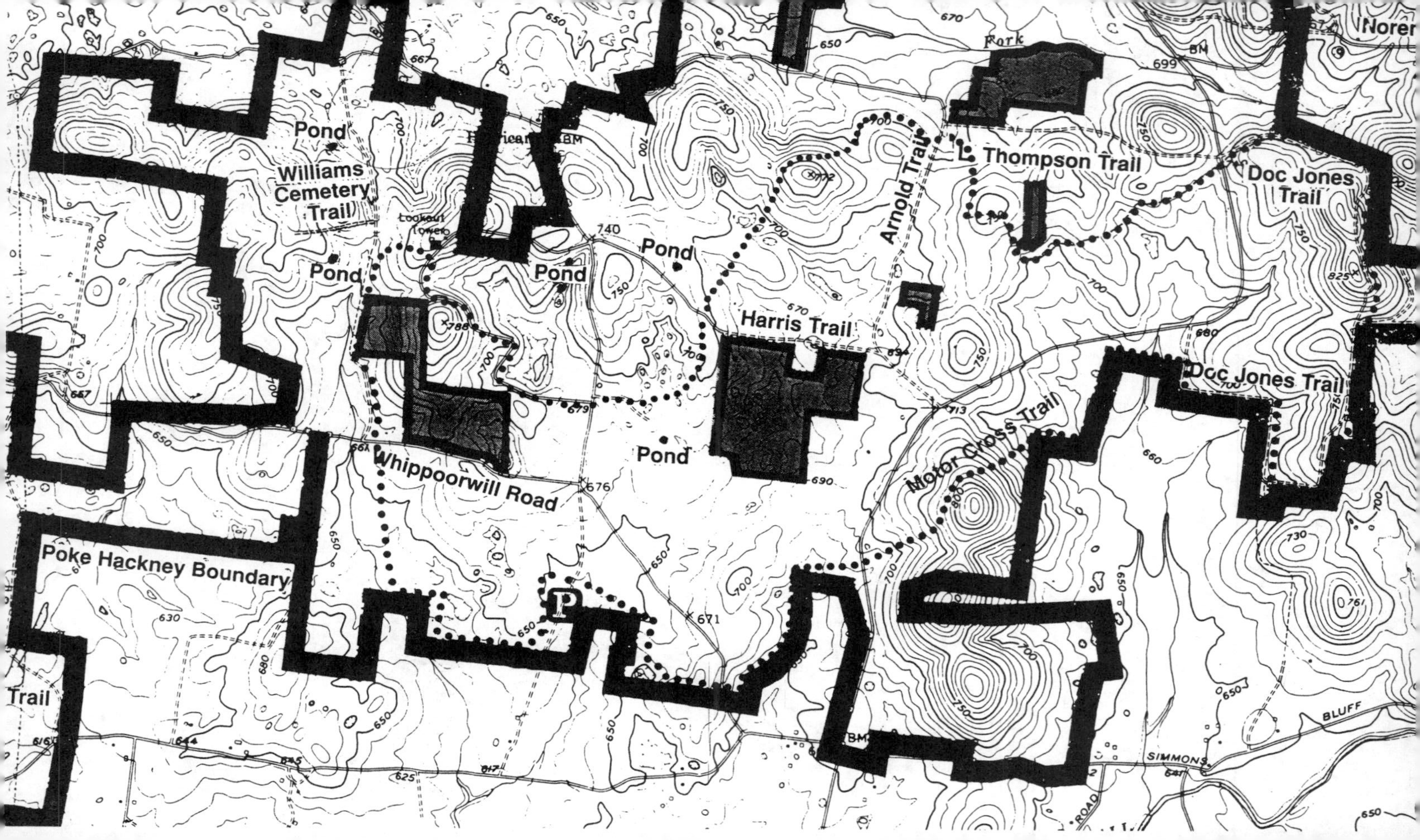

Pond
Williams Cemetery Trail
Lookout Tower
Pond
Pond
Pond
Pond
Arnold Trail
Thompson Trail
Doc Jones Trail
Harris Trail
Doc Jones Trail
Motor Cross Trail
Whippoorwill Road
Poke Hackney Boundary
Trail
Fork
Noren
SIMMONS
BLUFF
ROAD
P

CEDARS OF LEBANON S.F.

Cedars is divided into two parts: One is the State Park, the other is a State Forest. Until recently I thought most of the riding was accessed through the State Park. I was wrong. The State Forest is where we should be riding. There are no trails in the Park that are open for mountain biking.

The State Forest contains 9,000 acres of limestone glades and is one of the largest remaining stands of Red Cedars in the United States. There are many miles of trails and gravel roads available to ride on within the State Forest. The primary trail is a 12 mile off-road-vehicle trail that connects a number of roads and trails.

I don't have to tell those of you who have ridden here how rocky and rough it is. You will at times think you are riding on an abandoned rock quarry. There is also a noticeable lack of hills. Nowhere else in the state has a similar terrain. If you are interested in a new place to explore or are looking for a long trail that is not physically challenging, this is a good place to come. It is suitable for all riding levels. Be warned, the riding is very rough and rocky. It is my opinion that the other trails in this area are better suited to mountain biking.

There are several additional activities available at the State Park including a pool, frisbee golf or softball. There are cabins and camp sites and a camp store to buy supplies

Directions: Located between Murfreesboro and Lebanon on Hwy. 231. To get to the parking area at the State Forest continue south past the Park Headquarters 4.5 miles, turn left on Simmons Bluff Road. Drive 2.5 miles and turn left on Hurricane Mills Road (gravel) the trail head is a half mile up this road. If your coming from Murfreesboro, Simmons Bluff Road is the first right past the county line. For more information: Cedars of Lebanon S.F., Rt. 6 Box 220, Lebanon, TN 37087, 615-444-9394. Detailed maps are available.

CHATTANOOGA RIDING AREAS

Chattanooga is blessed with many places for mountain bikers to ride. You might want to check out the **Chickamunga National Battlefield**. This is a great beginner or intermediate riding area. It contains nearly 4,000 acres full of history and lots of trails and paths to ride. Better yet, we are welcome to ride here.

Raccoon Mountain is another large tract of land available for riding. I would suggest only the strong show up here. Most of the riding is not only steep, it's tough and technical.

Directions: The main road leading up is at the Alpine Slide on Raccoon Mountain. Get off at the Tiftonia exit and follow the signs. Warning: It is a nasty climb getting to the top. Once you reach it you have several riding options along the plateau.

Suck Creek: Located on the east side of Prentice Cooper is yet another small mountain full of jeep and single track trails. This falls under the same guidelines as all other W.M.A.s, so please be cautious of hunters.

Lookout Mountain: Just mention the name to anyone from this area and he or she will have a favorite spot on the mountain to ride. If you feel like exploring once you get past the city, you can start on just about any dirt road you see leading into the woods. There is a series of jeep, logging and four-wheeler trails throughout this area. Several years ago it was considered quite dangerous to venture into these parts. Today you are much safer. If you ride along the plateau, you will find moderate climbs and trails that are suitable for all riders. *(See the Five Points Story.)*

CHEATHAM W.M.A.

Located 45 minutes northeast of Nashville, you'll find nearly 35,000 acres of rolling hills and forests that are available with no riding restrictions. The area manager realizes mountain bicycles have little impact on the environment. He is happy to have us riding there, but prefers we do so only when hunting season is closed.

Cheatham W.M.A. has lots of jeep roads in various conditions. Many of these are very remote and offer a great back country experience. You'll have to do some riding on gravel roads, but this can be minimized once you know your way around.

Most of the riding would be considered intermediate. There are some long hills and lots of water crossings when in the valleys, most of which are shallow. The main attraction of this area is its size. We have done quite a bit of exploring and there's a lot left. It is possible to ride all day here and never have to back-track. Several areas have been logged recently, and trails we thought existed were dead-ends. Be sure to travel with a map and plenty of food and water.

The Brush Creek trail is where we generally ride. You can create a 10- to 15-mile loop with lots of scenery and some great ascents and descents plus several junctions to explore leading from the main trail. I recommend starting behind the headquarters and following this road to the T. Follow it left for a big downhill into the valley. Go left and cross the creek. Stay along the tree line for about a half mile. You will see a trail leading left uphill. Go right across the creek and follow the trail all the way up the valley. After the big climb at the end of the valley you will come to Brush Creek Road. To the left follows the ridge then leads downhill to the trail you rode past in the valley. Ride backward from that point back to your car. If you turn right at the end of the valley, you will end up back on the main road turn left on it to return to the Park Headquarters. The trails that lead north from the valley will take you to Wiley Pardue Rd.

Directions: From Nashville, take I-24 east to exit 24. Take Rt. 49 through Ashland City and across the bridge (approximately three miles). Hwy. 250 spurs off to the left. Follow it for 7-8 miles and look for a country store and fire tower. You can park here or drive to the headquarters. If you take the gravel road south and split left, it will take you to the park headquarters. You can access the southern half of the park conveniently by parking at the Narrows of the Harpeth off Hwy. 70 near Belleview. Backtrack up the road for about 200 yards and follow the jeep road to the left.

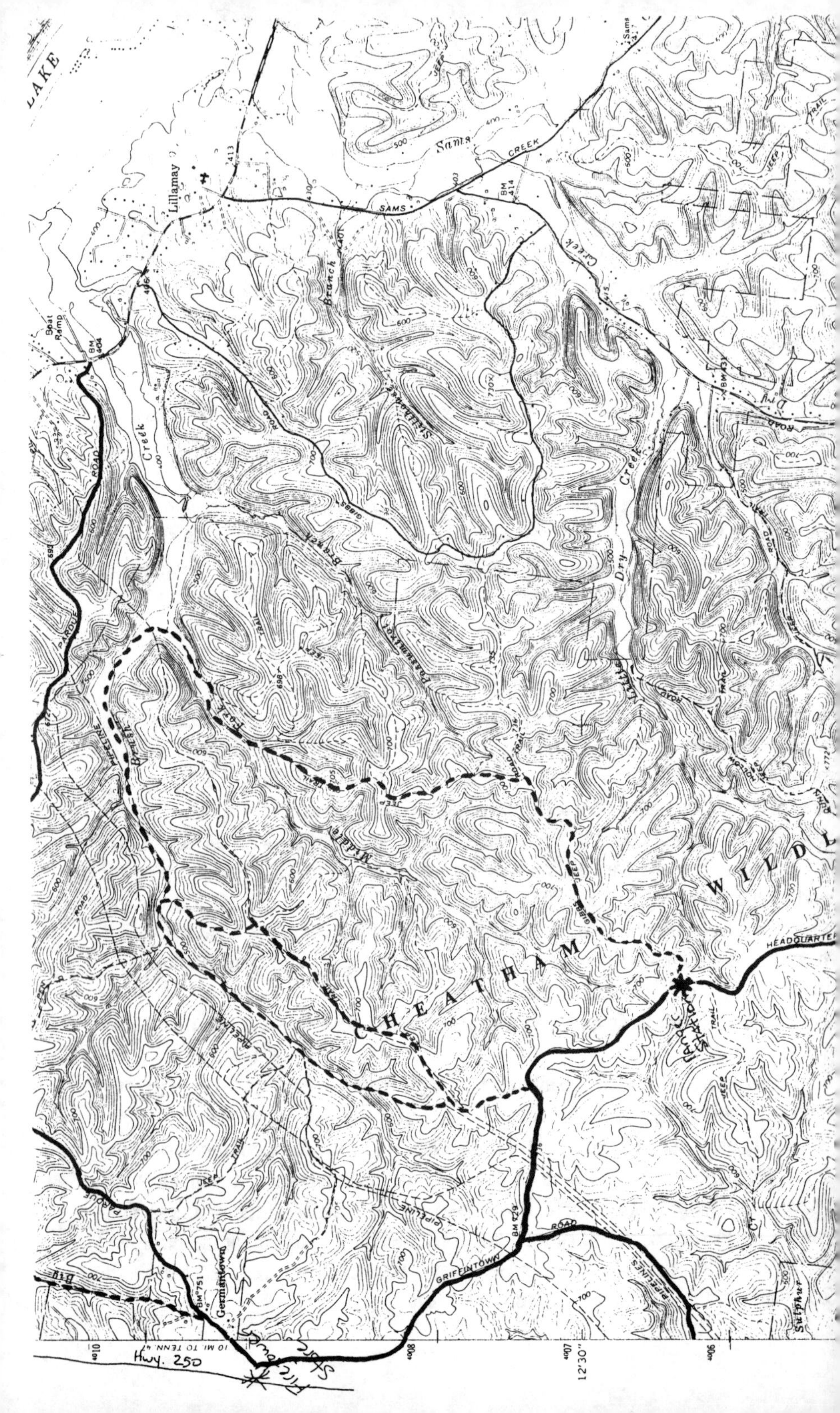

LAKE
Sams Creek
SAMS
Lillamay
Boat Ramp
Creek
Branch
Stillhouse
GIBBS
Branch
Dry Creek
Little Dry Creek
PARDUE ROAD
PIPELINE
Brush
Fork
Middle
CHEATHAM
WILDL
HEADQUARTERS
GRIFFINTOWN ROAD
Germantown
PIPELINES
Sulphur
10 MI. TO TENN. 47
Hwy. 250
12'30"

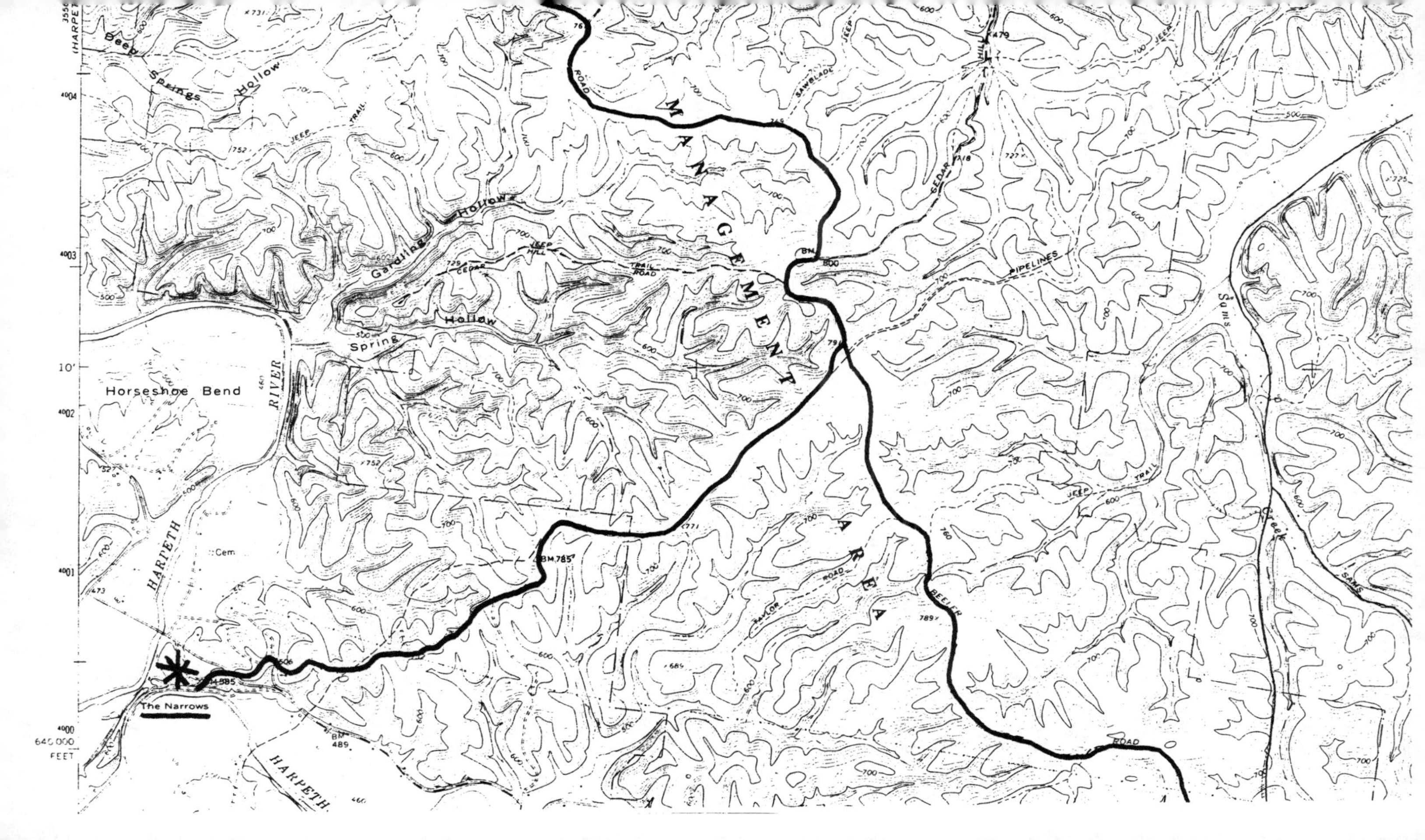

Deep Springs Hollow
Gardline Hollow
Spring Hollow
M A N A G E M E N T
A R E A
ROAD
SAWBLADE
JEEP TRAIL
CEDAR
HILL
JEEP HILL
CEDAR
TRAIL ROAD
PIPELINES
Sams
Creek
SAMS
BEELER
ROAD
TAYLOR ROAD
Horseshoe Bend
RIVER
HARPETH
HARPETH
Cem
BM 785
BM 489
The Narrows
4004
4003
10'
4002
4001
4000
645 000
FEET

CHEROKEE NATIONAL FOREST

Cherokee has more than 600,000 acres available to us from Chattanooga to Bristol. With the exception of the Smokies, it runs along the entire border between Tennessee and North Carolina. This is a multi-use area like our State Forests, so hunting, logging, mining, and other activities are going on throughout the year.

I spoke with the park headquarters about mountain biking in the National Forest and, with the exception of hiking trails and wilderness areas, we have full access. There are a number of *closed gate* roads we may use also. Cherokee is divided up into five specific districts. Each area is so large I'm not able to provide maps. Contact the district offices to request a copy.

Hiwassee Ranger District, PO Drawer D, Etowah, TN 37331, 423-263-5486. This district offers more than 260 miles of paved and unpaved roads. The Hiwassee area is between Ocoee and the Smoky Mountains National Park.

Nolichucky Ranger District, 120 Austin Ave., Greeneville, TN 37743, 423-638-4109. Here you'll find more than 100 miles of roads. Bikers are not allowed on the Appalachian Trail. This is the section just north of the Smokies.

Ocoee Ranger District, Rt. 1 Box 348D, Benton, TN 37307, 423-338-5201. Here you'll find more than 100 miles of unpaved roads that are open to mountain bikes. This district is making great strides to accommodate mountain bikes. Lots of hiking trails have been opened to us and they are planning to build additional trails near the river. Call the district and ask them about new areas that may have developed since this book was updated. While you're here, go by an outfitter and run the Ocoee River. It's a raft trip you won't soon forget.

Unaka Ranger District, 1205 North Main St., Erwin, TN 37650 423-743-4452. With more than 125 miles of unpaved roads, mountain bikers can spend days up here without seeing the same views. The Rock Creek Park loop is highly recommended to ride while you're here. This section is located between the Nolichucky and Watauga Districts.

Watauga Ranger District, Rt. 9 Box 2235, Elizabethon, TN 37643, 423-542-2942. This area in the Northeastern corner of Tennessee also offers miles of endless jeep roads waiting to be explored.

CADES COVE

This is a must for every bike rider in Tennessee. Cades Cove is a valley in the heart of the Smokies that is not only beautiful, it's extremely peaceful. You've probably driven around here in your car during your last vacation. After the first 100 yards on your bike, you'll realize how much you missed behind the car windows.

For those of you who've never visited, you'll find an 11-mile paved loop that resembles a petting farm nestled among the Smoky Mountains. If you take a morning or afternoon ride, you'll see more deer than you can count. You'll find all kinds of wildlife here, and of course the beautiful mountains and the sounds and smells that go along with them. Riders of all abilities will enjoy this loop. There are some small hills to ride up and shortcuts are available.

Cades Cove is also a historical area. Take time to explore the homesteads of the families that called this valley home 100 years ago. Halfway around the Cove is a replica of a working farm. It makes you appreciate the simpler things in life.

Directions: Follow 321 south of Maryville through Townsend. Once you enter, the National Park signs are posted. It's about an hour from Knoxville, or 40 minutes from Gatlinburg depending on traffic. I would suggest riding early or late in the day since this is a popular place for tourists. The gates close at dusk and open at 10:30 on Saturday mornings, providing a quiet time for walkers and cyclists. During full moons you can join the Appalachian bicycle club for a moonlit ride around the cove.

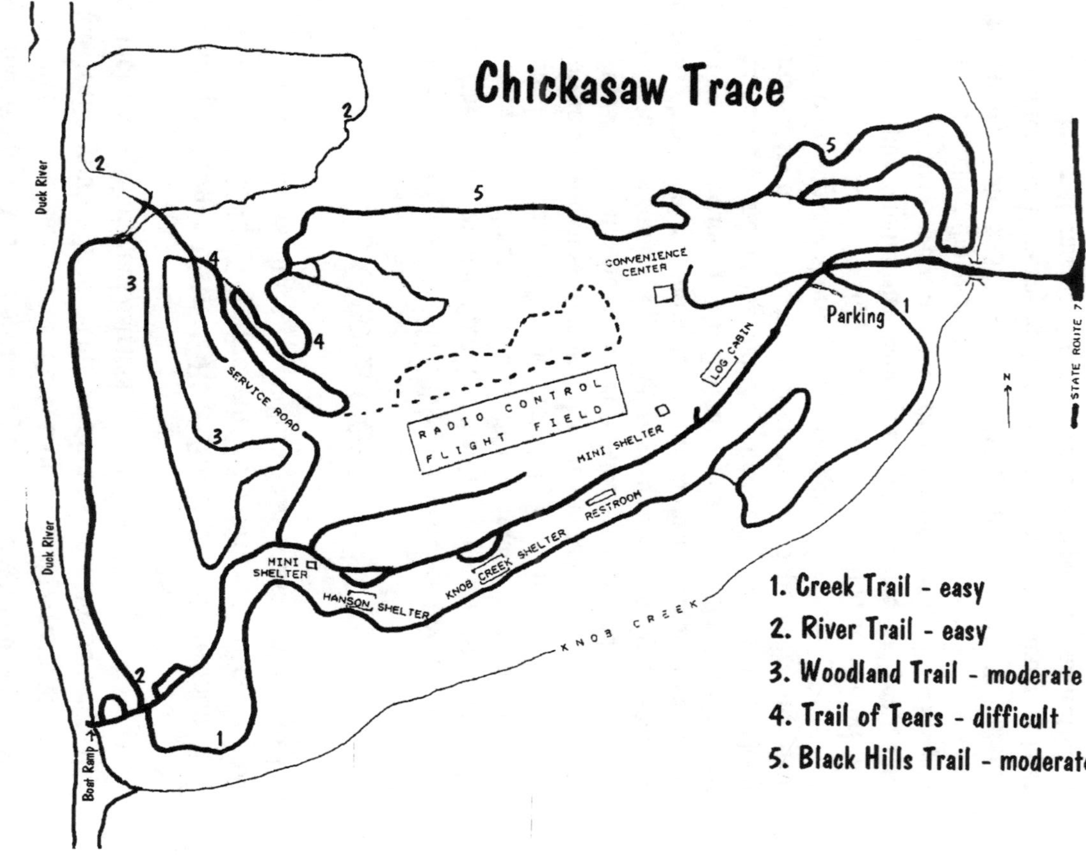
Chickasaw Trace
Duck River
Duck River
Boat Ramp
MINI SHELTER
HANSON SHELTER
KNOB CREEK SHELTER
RESTROOM
MINI SHELTER
SERVICE ROAD
RADIO CONTROL
FLIGHT FIELD
CONVENIENCE CENTER
LOG CABIN
Parking
KNOB CREEK
STATE ROUTE 7
N
1. Creek Trail - easy
2. River Trail - easy
3. Woodland Trail - moderate
4. Trail of Tears - difficult
5. Black Hills Trail - moderate

Chickasaw Trace

Located just outside of Columbia, TN, Nashville riders just got another option for a good local place to ride. Built by the Columbia Bicycle Club, it was made to be ridden. Better yet, all types of riders can learn, enjoy and find lots of challenges along the 6+ miles of singletrack already built, and several more miles of trails are planned as additional access is provided across the river.

There are five main trail sections. The Creek and River trails run along Knob Creek, then follow the banks of the Duck River to a new loop section along the back of the park. Most of the riding in the lowlands and is relatively flat with a few technical areas. Beginners can make a nice 5-6 mile loop to hone their skills. Once you reach the Woodland trail you get into rolling singletrack winding below and up a long ridge. You drop back down towards the river and begin what seems like a non-ending series of climbs up and down the "Trail of Tears." It only looks like three climbing sections but I would swear it is really eight. You will be hurting when you finish this section.

There is a new trail planned off the "Trail of Tears" that may break up the climbing and add another mile to the overall loop. When you reach the last climb you will find yourself in a gravel/rocky area that you are happy to leave. This is an active landfill and you will ride past parts of it. No smelly garbage, just stuff. Dropping down from this area you're back into the woods for more fun rolling, tight riding down the ridge to Knob Creek. A few more climbs and tight descents and you're back to the car.

Riding counterclockwise makes the climbs seem easier but it will take longer to complete a lap. Chickasaw Trace offers the singletrack of Hamilton Creek without the rocks. Go down and ride it, this may turn into your favorite riding spot. It's that good.

Directions: From Nashville take 65 south and exit on Saturn Parkway. When you enter Columbia, turn west on the by-pass (412,43) and go one mile. Exit on Hwy. 7, drive north 3.1 miles and Chickasaw Trace will be on your left. Park down in the valley.

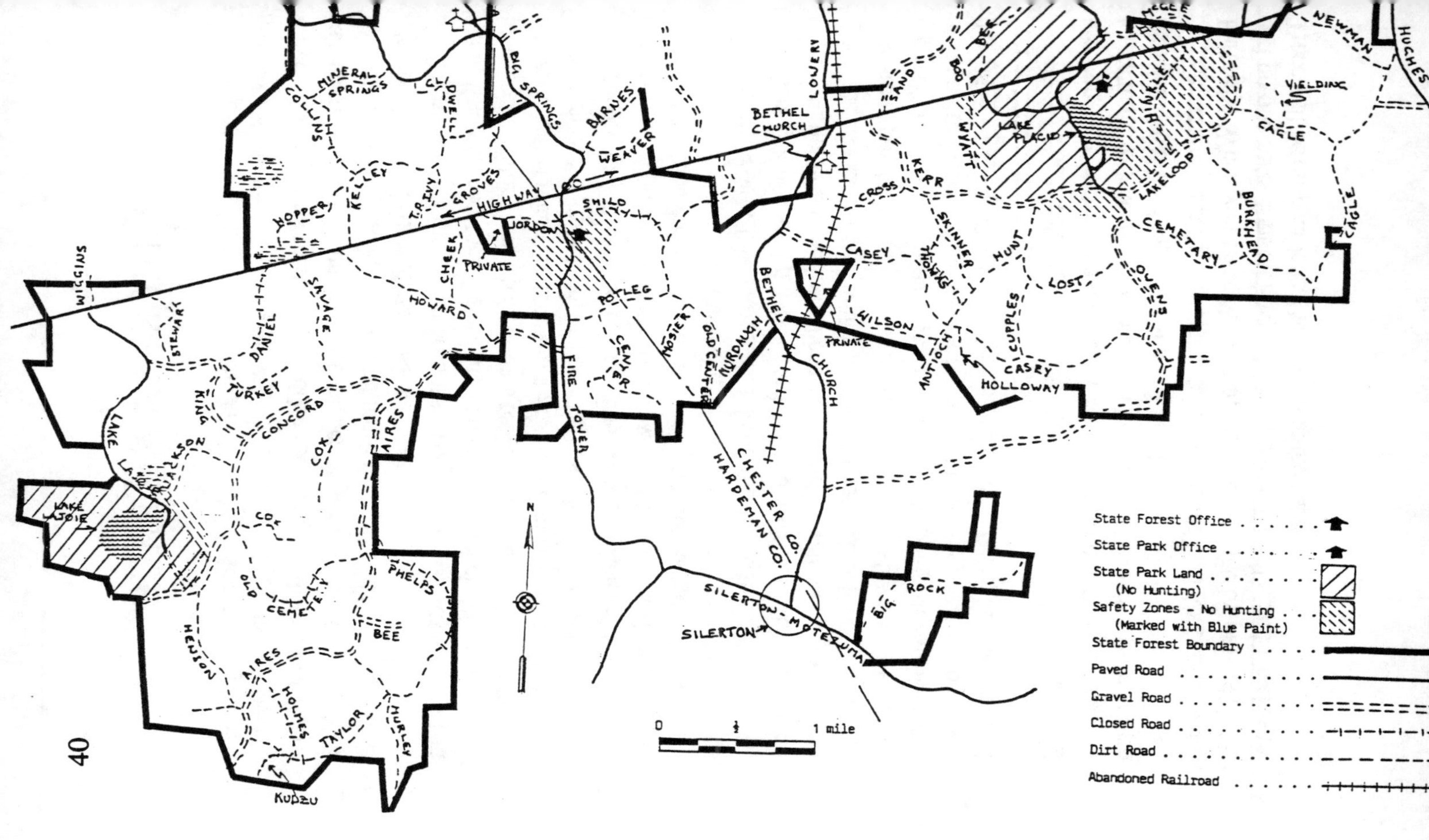
State Forest Office
State Park Office
State Park Land (No Hunting)
Safety Zones - No Hunting (Marked with Blue Paint)
State Forest Boundary
Paved Road
Gravel Road
Closed Road
Dirt Road
Abandoned Railroad
0
½
1 mile
N
HIGHWAY 100
CHESTER CO.
HARDEMAN CO.
SILERTON
SILERTON - MOTEZUMA
BIG ROCK
FIRE TOWER
LAKE LAJOIE
LAKE PLACID
BETHEL CHURCH
LOWERY
WIGGINS
STEWART
DANIEL
SAVAGE
HOWARD
CHEEK
PRIVATE
JORDON
SHILO
POTLEG
CENTER
MOSIER
OLD CENTER
MURDAUGH
BETHEL
CHURCH
WILSON
ANTIOCH
CASEY
HOLLOWAY
CUPPLES
LOST
HUNT
SKINNER
KERR
CROSS
OWENS
CEMETARY
BURKHEAD
LAKELOOP
HINKLE
CAGLE
VIELDING
NEWMAN
HUGHES
MCGEE
BEE
BOO
SAND
WYATT
MINERAL SPRINGS
COLLINS
CL DWELL
BIG SPRINGS
BARNES
WEAVER
KELLEY
HOPPER
T.R. IVY
GROVES
KING
TURKEY
CONCORD
COX
AIRES
LAKE
JACKSON
OLD CEMETERY
PHELPS
HENSON
HOLMES
TAYLOR
HURLEY
KUDZU

CHICKASAW STATE FOREST

Chickasaw's 14,384 acres are situated on some of the highest terrain in West Tennessee. Managed by the Division of Forestry and the TWRA, you'll find a variety of activities including a picturesque beach on Lake Placid. Rowboats are available, and the fishing is great. There is also camping, lakeside cabins, and a restaurant on site.

Mountain bikers will find more than 50 miles of back country roads and horse trails to explore. It is a network that offers an unlimited combination of loops. This park is similar to the Natchez Trace S.P. in that we are welcome to all the trails at our convenience, excluding their hiking trails.

I spoke with the Superintendent who encouraged us to use Chickasaw's trails. He did caution that equestrians also use the trails. Located just 18 miles south of Jackson on Hwy. 100, Chickasaw provides a convenient area to ride for most West Tennesseans. A fully equipped group lodge large enough for 40 persons is available year round.

For more information, contact the Chickasaw State Park, Henderson, TN 38340, 901- 989-5141

HELPFUL HINT

When installing new grips, clean your bar with *Windex*, then slide the grips on while the bar is still wet. It dries quickly and won't slip. Hair spray (used sparingly) also works well.

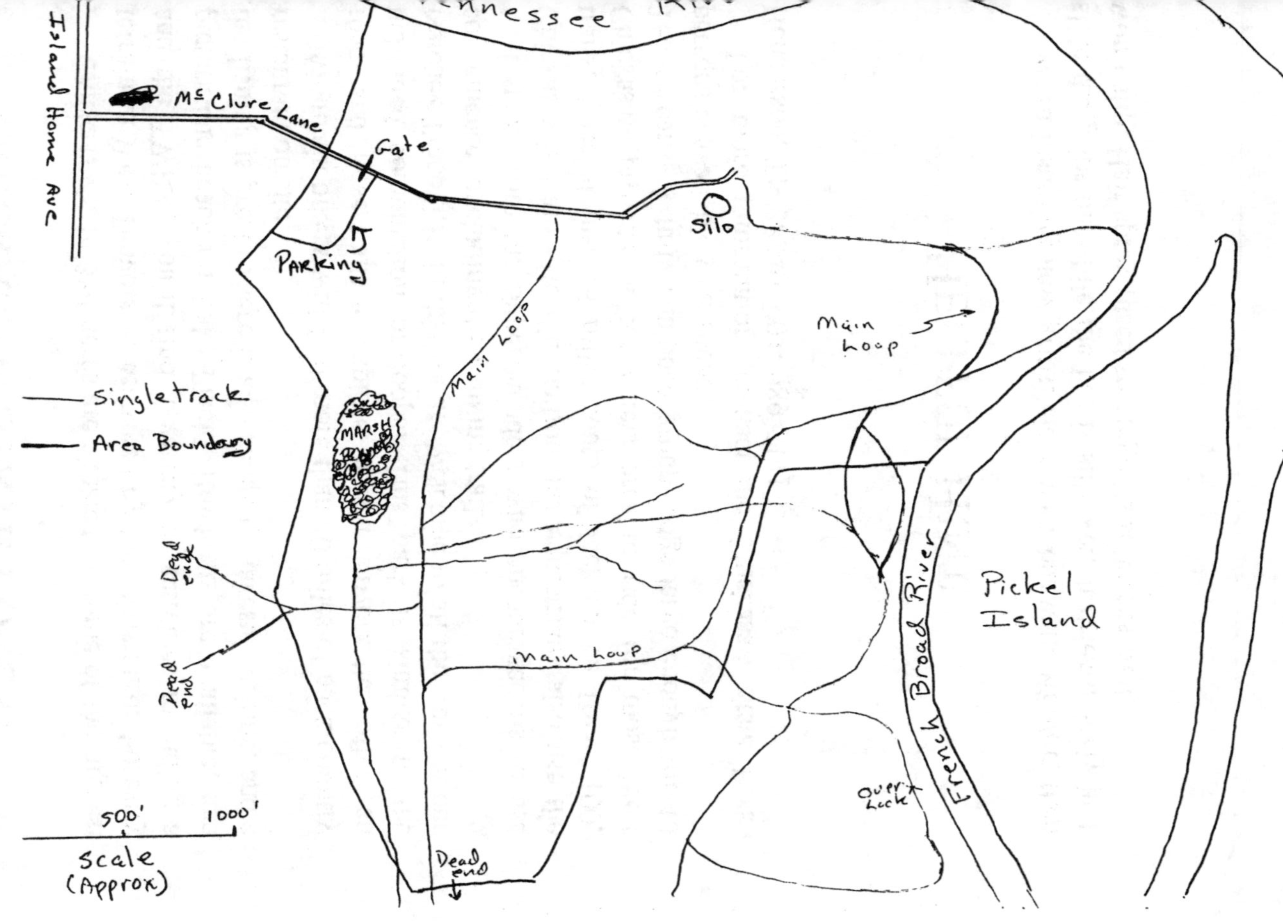
Island Home Ave
McClure Lane
Gate
Parking
Silo
Main Loop
Main Loop
Main Loop
Singletrack
Area Boundary
MARSH
Dead end
Dead end
Dead end
Overlook
French Broad River
Pickel Island
500'
1000'
Scale
(Approx)

EASTERN STATE WMA

This 350-acre Wildlife Management Area near downtown Knoxville has a great network of trails, most of which are single-track with several rocky and rutted technical sections. The climbs are all short, but some are quite steep. Located on the shores of the Tennessee River, the scenery is great and there are several overlooks to the water below.

The vegetation is varied and quite interesting. A small marsh is filled with cat-tails and an abundance of wildlife. Nearby on a dry hillside you will find small cactus. Primarily a hardwood forest with overgrown clearings, as with most WMAs, you are likely to experience a variety of fauna.

It is not recommended that you ride here during wet conditions. Not only is it hard on the trails, here you are met with slippery, sticky mud that will stop you in your tracks.

Trails are closed periodically from September 1 through March 1 for hunting season. As with all Wildlife Management Areas, hunters have priority because the land and all its upkeep is paid for through their hunting licenses.

Directions: From I-40 in Knoxville, exit on U.S. 441 south and go .9 miles. Immediately after crossing the Tennessee River turn left onto Blount Avenue. Go .2 miles. Turn right at the second light onto Sevier Avenue and go another .7 miles. Turn left on Island Home Avenue for 2.7 miles. There are several sharp turns. Turn left on McClure Lane and the trailhead is in .4 miles.

Thanks to Danny Gray for contributing this story and map.

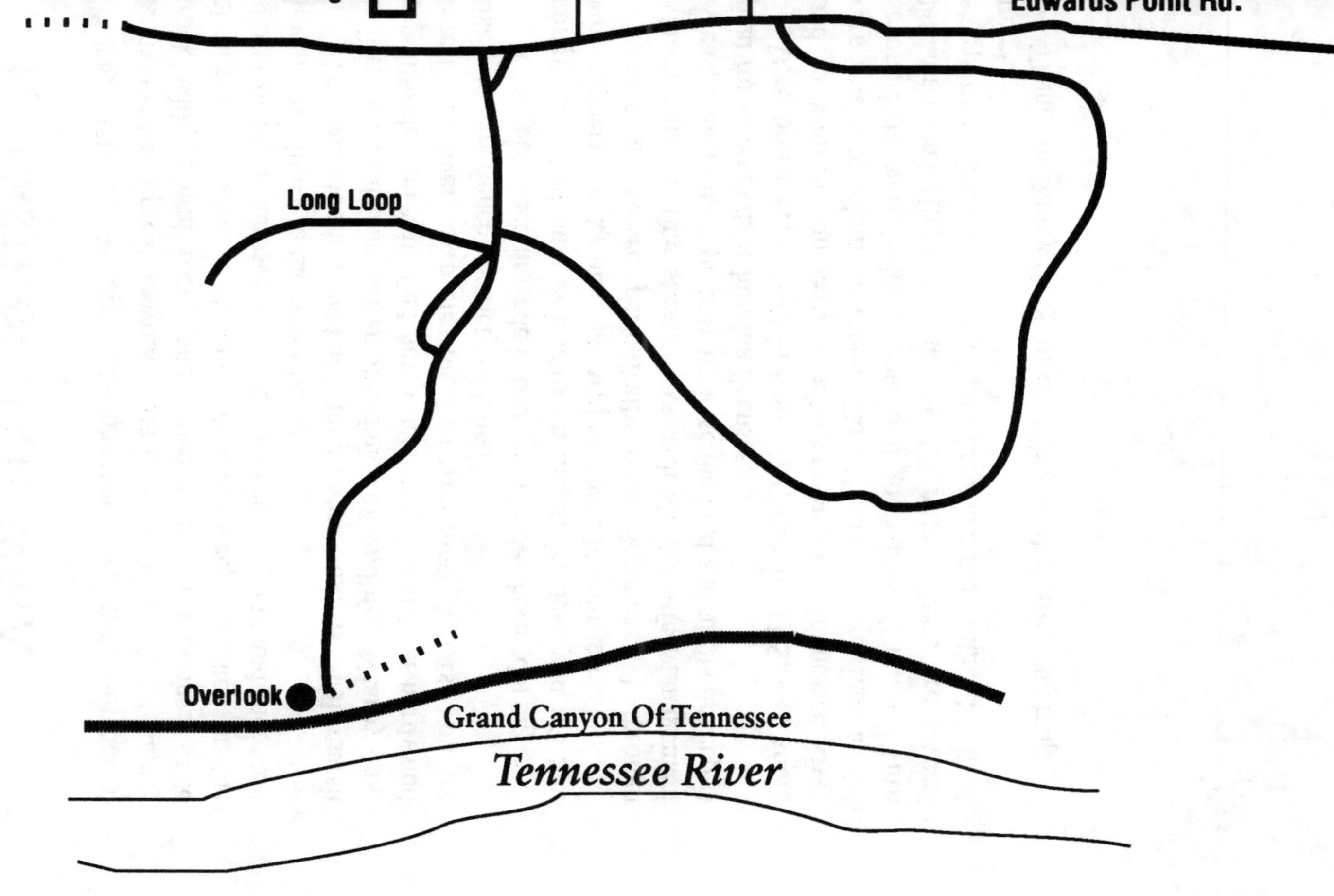
Edwards Point Rd.
Long Loop
Overlook
Grand Canyon Of Tennessee
Tennessee River

EDWARD'S POINT

This Chattanooga ride will take you to a lookout over the Grand Canyon of Tennessee. Located atop Signal Mountain are mountain bike trails that all levels of riders will enjoy.

The main trail is about three miles long with just a few moderate climbs. The reward is at the end of the trail. You will be perched high atop the Tennessee River looking into a beautiful gorge. Follow the hiking trail along the bluff to your left. This will lead you to two waterfalls.

You can find several side trips to amuse yourself. First, the long trip. About halfway back you will see a four-way intersection. If you follow the trail leading west, you have nearly 15 more miles of trails ahead of you. This will lead you through some old mining areas, more beautiful overlooks, and the world famous (not really) mushroom rock. It is a 15-foot-tall rock formation that looks like a big mushroom. This trail eventually leads you back to Edward's Point Road just a few hundred yards from the Sportsman's lodge.

The single-track lovers will want to continue back toward your car for another 100 yards. Look for a big berm blocking off a four-wheeler trail on the right. This is it: four miles of fun ascents and descents. Look for some smaller trails leading to the east. They will lead back to the waterfalls. This trail ends up on Edward's Road. If you park on Edward's at the intersection with two stone walls, the trail is a couple hundred yards back up the road. Go this way for a 30-mph downhill that will really take your breath away.

Directions: From Chattanooga, drive up Signal Mountain. As you reach the top, just before the traffic light, turn left on Signal Mountain Blvd. It will turn into James Blvd. at the top of the hill. Continue up and turn left on Timberlinks just before the golf course. This will turn into Edward's Point Rd. Follow it for 3.5 miles and park at the Waldens Ridge Sportmans Lodge. The trail is back down the road about 50 feet on your right.

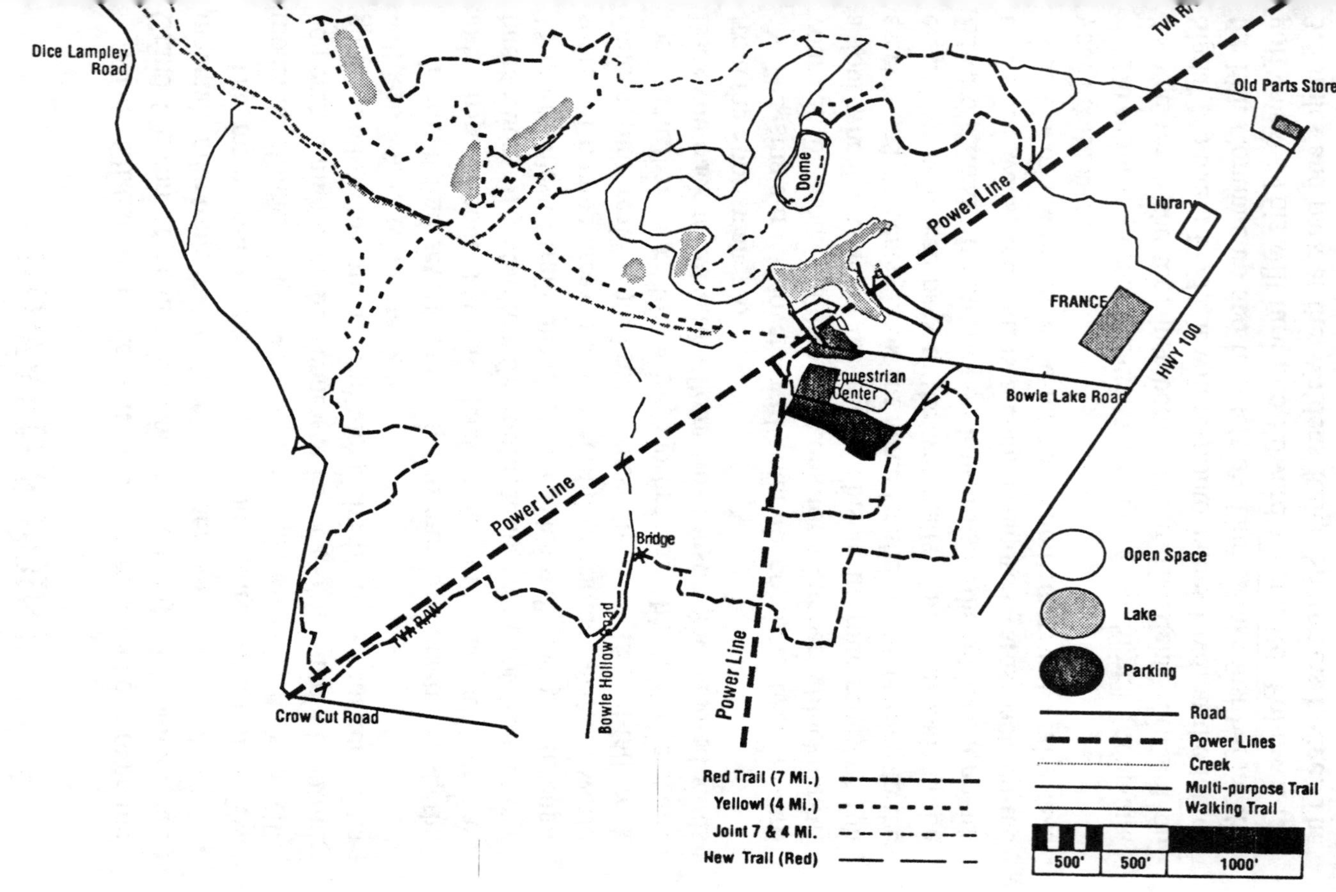

Dice Lampley Road
TVA R/W
Old Parts Store
Dome
Power Line
Library
FRANCE
HWY 100
Equestrian Center
Bowie Lake Road
Power Line
Bridge
TVA R/W
Bowie Hollow Road
Power Line
Crow Cut Road
Open Space
Lake
Parking
Road
Power Lines
Creek
Multi-purpose Trail
Walking Trail
Red Trail (7 Mi.)
Yellowl (4 Mi.)
Joint 7 & 4 Mi.
New Trail (Red)
500'
500'
1000'

FAIRVIEW NATURE PARK

Fairview is currently one of the most popular places to ride in Middle Tennessee. If you've been there you know why: It's lots of fun. The trails are in great shape whether it's wet or dry. They're long enough so you aren't bored just going 'round and 'round. It seems no matter when you go there you'll find someone to ride with. (Do bike riders ever work? Stop by on a nice day and you will wonder.)

Fairview also has been home to several races, and I hear there are more in the making as well. If you like to go fast, you can do it. There are several hills, but they're gradual enough that beginners can ride up, and experts run the big ring. In 1993, a seven-mile loop was laid out which is challenging enough to keep even the hotshots interested.

Keep in mind when you ride here that the horses were here first. Most of us drive in from other counties; the folks on the horses live here. They pay the taxes and have ridden here for years. **Please** when you encounter horses, get off your bike and let them by. If you see someone riding recklessly around horses, remember it will only take one accident to ruin things for all of us. We must patrol ourselves.

Directions: From Nashville take I-40 west to Hwy. 96. Go south to Hwy. 100 and drive west for 1.3 miles. Look for a business called *FRANCE* on the right. You'll turn on Bowie Lake Road just past their sign. Parking and picnic areas are at the bottom of the hill.

Don't skid.

Skidmarks are mountain bike litter.

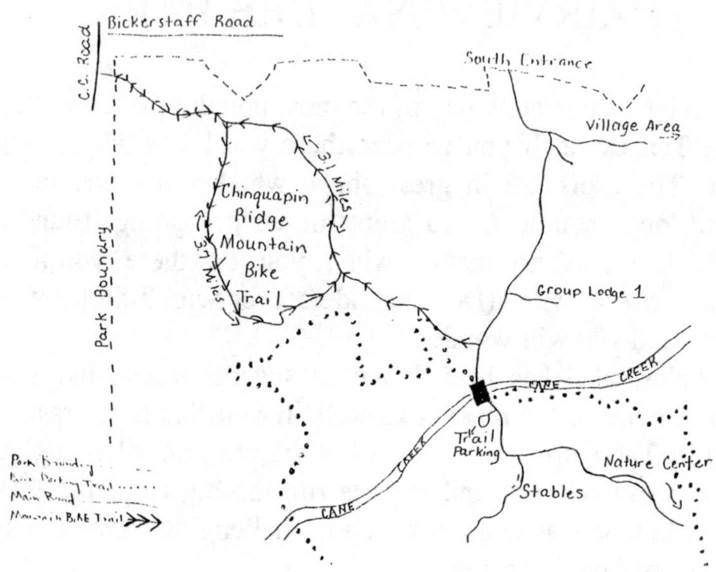

Bickerstaff Road
C.C. Road
South Entrance
Village Area
3.1 Miles
Chinquapin Ridge Mountain Bike Trail
3.7 Miles
Park Boundry
Group Lodge 1
CANE CREEK
Trail Parking
Nature Center
Stables

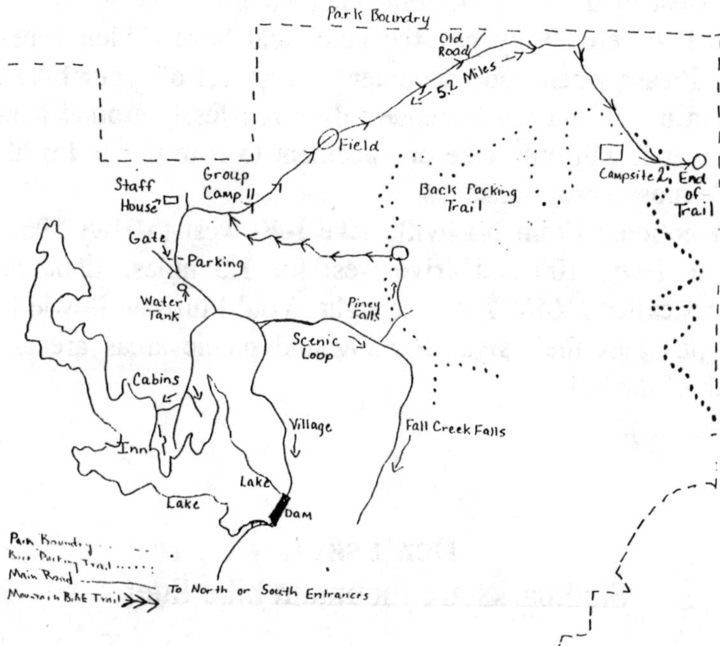

Park Boundry
Old Road
5.2 Miles
Field
Staff House
Group Camp II
Back Packing Trail
Campsite 2
End of Trail
Gate
Parking
Water Tank
Piney Falls
Scenic Loop
Cabins
Village
Fall Creek Falls
Inn
Lake
Lake
Dam
Main Road
To North or South Entrances

FALL CREEK FALLS S.P.

Located on the western edge of the Cumberland Plateau, Fall Creek Falls State Park is one of the most scenic recreation areas in Tennessee. Until recently we have been banned from using the fire and access roads within the park. Luckily, some of the rangers like to ride and are opening the park for our use.

Currently there are two trails available for mountain bikers. The Cane Creek Trail is an easy out-and-back trip all riders will enjoy. It is a logging road in good condition and should be a great trail for first time-riders. The Chinquapin Ridge trail runs along the southern end of the park. It is in a remote area offering a more challenging trail. Be sure you carry a map on this trail because there are several junctions. Maps are available at the ranger station and visitors center. There is also a four-mile paved loop available leading past the lake and several scenic overlooks.

Fall Creek Falls is a family destination, and they are looking forward to providing new recreational services for the nearly one million visitors they receive each year. Maps are available. In the future, they hope to have rental mountain bikes available.

Fall Creek Falls is home to the highest waterfalls east of the Rocky Mountains at 256 feet. Other falls within the park include Piney and Cane Creek falls and Cane Creek cascades. If you hike down into Cane Creek Gorge, it's some of the last virgin timber in the area due to its remote location. There are also several hiking and backpacking trails throughout the park. The hiking trails are closed to mountain bikes.

Directions: From Cookeville take Hwy. 111 south through Sparta until you reach Spencer. From here follow Hwy. 30 east for 11 miles, go right on Hwy. 284 into the park. Signs are posted. For information, call 615-881-3297.

FIVE POINTS ON LOOKOUT MTN.

Located atop Lookout Mountain overlooking Chattanooga is one on the largest networks of off-road trails available to mountain bikers. Technically, you are in Georgia, but that's OK. I call this area Five Points.

Follow this jeep road for about a mile and you will reach the Five Points intersection. Now it is decision time. The first trail to the right leads to a power line and a house. You might want to start on another. The second is a beautiful ride along the ridges. When you reach the power lines, you have three options. I climbed the steep hill to the right back under the lines. After reaching the top it is a fun single-track downhill which completes a three-mile loop back to Five Points. With the exception of one steep climb, this is a trail everyone will enjoy.

I found the middle trail to be the most extreme. It was mostly four-wheeler trails and had lots of chutes and woop-de-doos. After several miles it connected to a jeep road and finally ended on a paved road. When you reach the power lines, turn left and follow the first trail leading back into the woods. After some technical climbing and a fun downhill you will once again be at Five Points. This is about a six-mile loop. Again, there are several additional trails that lead off these main trails you can explore for longer trips. There are some steep climbs and rocky sections on this trail, but for the most part riders of all abilities should enjoy these trails.

The fourth trail from the right is a fun and very scenic trip, one I call the Ridge Runner. It is about six miles of fairly easy riding offering deep valley views. Once you reach the top of the mountain, you are rewarded with a beautiful overlook of the plateau. Then a fun downhill leads you back to Five Points. The last trail is where the four-wheeler and ridge runner trails exit.

Directions: Once you reach the city of Lookout Mountain, follow Rock City signs until you reach the Rock City turn-off. Continue on Luna Lake for 10.4 miles. You will pass Eddie's Market, then in about 1-2 miles, Mt. Pleasant cemetery will be on your left. This is the parking area. Ride about 75 yards further up the road and you will see the trailhead on the right.

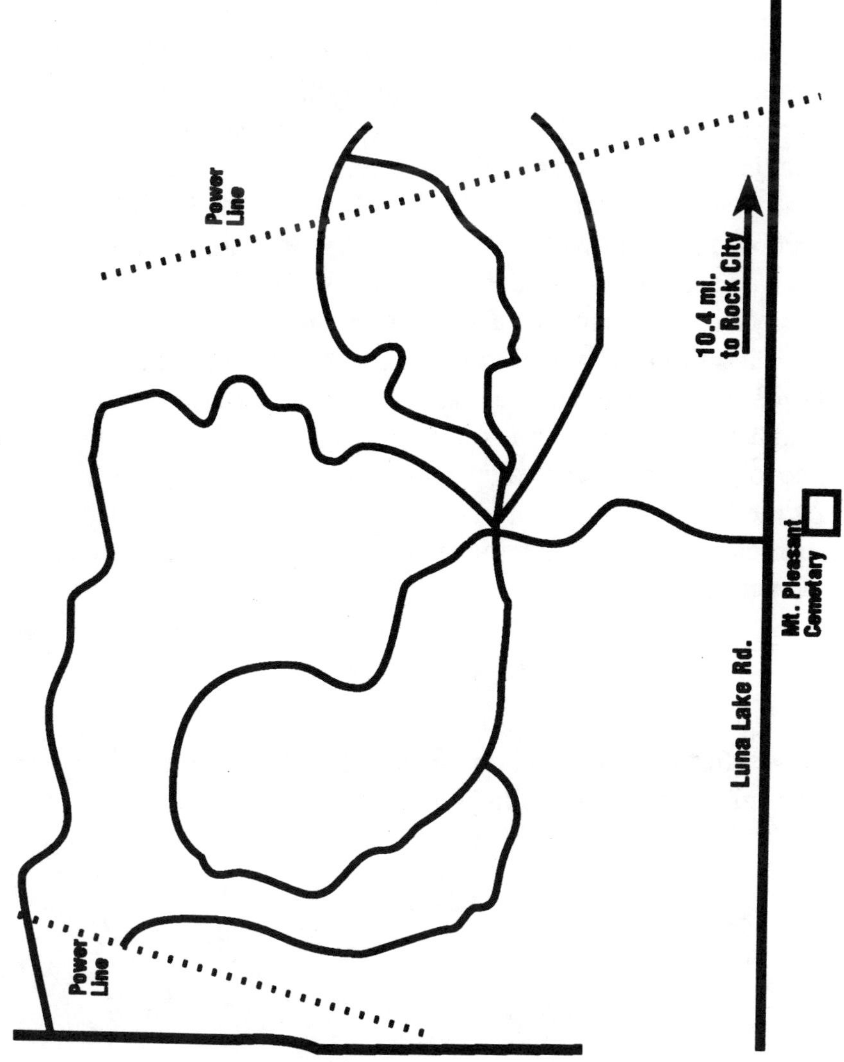

Fort Campbell ORV Trails

Fort Campbell includes huge tracts of land in Tennessee and Kentucky. In many cases, we are not allowed on the property. However, the soldiers have some land to play on, and the ORV trails are just that. Located on the outskirts of Clarksville is a maze of roller coaster trails that until now have only been ridden by the local mountain bikers and hair scramblers.

At this point, you will find a series of connecting trails. If you start on the right, this trail will lead you around the perimeter of the park. Once you reach the parking lot there are additional trails across the gravel road. There is a small gravel road you follow for about a half mile that leads you to the hilly section. Here you will find lots of rollers that are short and steep.

The motorcycles and four-wheelers have created great trails and berms for fast riding and lots of whoop-de-doos.

Directions: From downtown Clarksville, take Ft. Campbell Blvd. north, then turn left at the signal just before you reach Walmart. When you reach the stop sign near North West High School, turn right and follow this road to the left when it splits. At the four-way stop, turn right and then turn on the first gravel road on your left. Watch for the motorcycle/ORV signs that mark the parking area.

Helpful Hints

Power Bar wrappers and dollar bills do a great job repairing torn sidewalls. Keep an extra in your fanny pack.

FRANKLIN STATE FOREST

This hilly and rugged section of the Cumberland Plateau just south of Sewanee consists of nearly 7,000 acres. You'll discover some beautiful yet very demanding trails. Much of the area has good jeep roads that provide access to many remote areas.

I suggest riding the Franklin Forest Trail. This is a beautiful hiking trail the Boy Scouts recently improved. Starting at the lookout tower, you ride east to the rim of a beautiful gorge. The main trail goes left and follows the rim for seven miles to the north. There is a new trail to the right you should try on the way out if you have an extra 45 minutes. It has a great climb at the end and really makes for a tough ride.

At mile 3.2 you will reach a four-way intersection. If you continue on the main trail you will descend along the bluffs for nearly a mile. Although the scenery is excellent, the trail is unrideable and you will carry your bike through most of this section. I recommend you turn left at the intersection and follow the yellow flags to the right. Another rider has laid out a trail that stays above the ridge and joins back up with the main trail where it is again rideable. You also can follow the jeep road left, then stay to the right at each intersection. Watch for a small connector trail that is flagged 3/4 of a mile on the right.

The main trail continues for another mile and a half then joins the North Rim Trail. A left turn here will take you to the rangers station. The North Rim Trail is fun rolling singletrack with plenty of overlooks. The main trail ends in 2.5 miles; recent horse travelers have added some additional trails but they all end in dead ends.

If you stay above the rim, the riding is suitable for all abilities. Water is available at the ranger station.

Directions: Exit I-24 at Monteagle, take Hwy. 64 west to Hwy. 156. Then go south on 156 for about 8 miles and you'll enter the State Forest. Park at the fire tower; the trail leads from there and is marked in white. For more information, call Clint Stromeier, the forester for this area at 615-967-0757 or 598-5507.

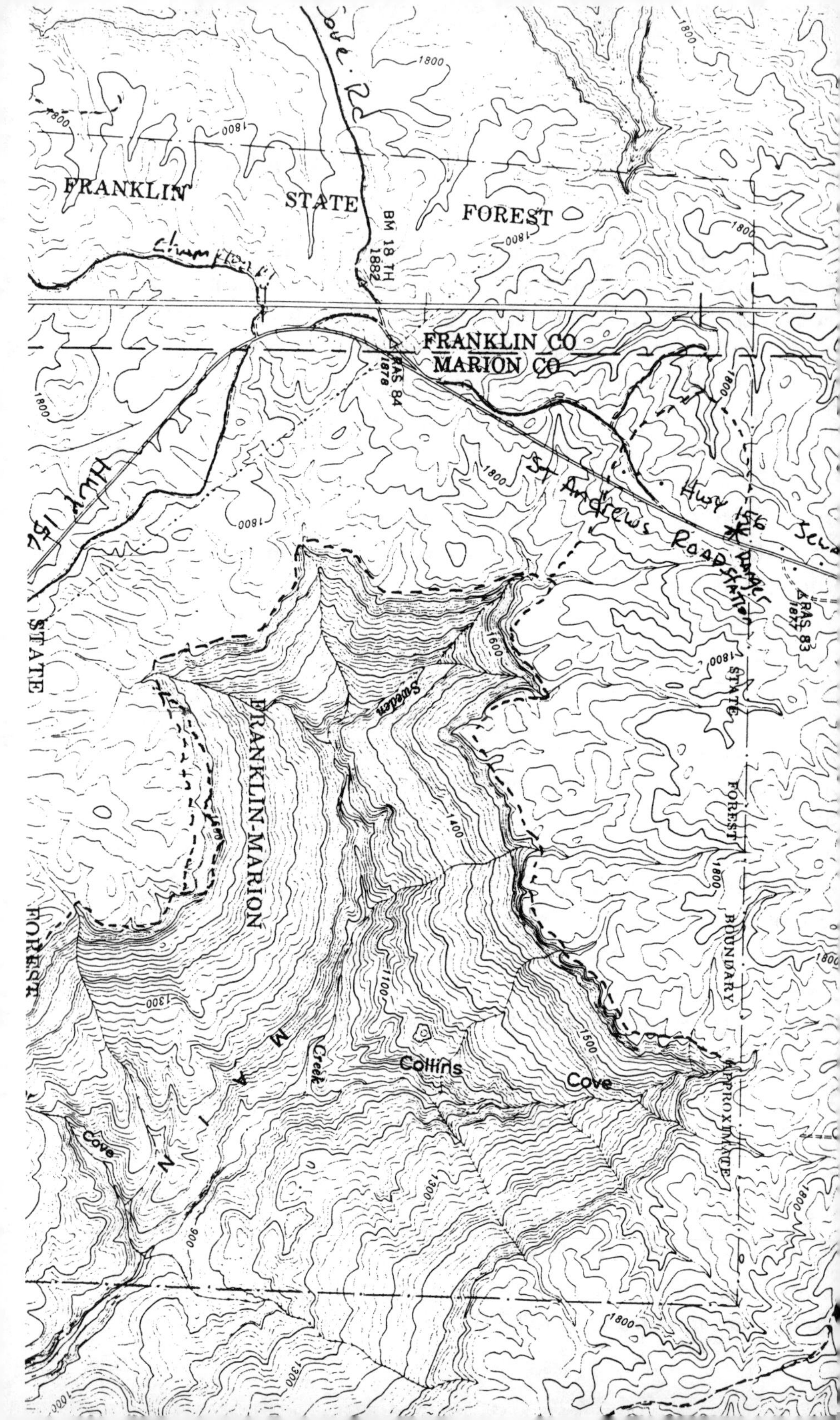

FRANKLIN
STATE
FOREST
BM 18 TH
1882
FRANKLIN CO
MARION CO
RAS 84
1878
RAS 83
1877
Hwy 156
St Andrews Road Station
Danger
STATE
FOREST
BOUNDARY
APPROXIMATE
FRANKLIN-MARION
STATE
FOREST
Collins
Cove
Creek
Cove
1800
1600
1400
1300
1100
1500
900
1000

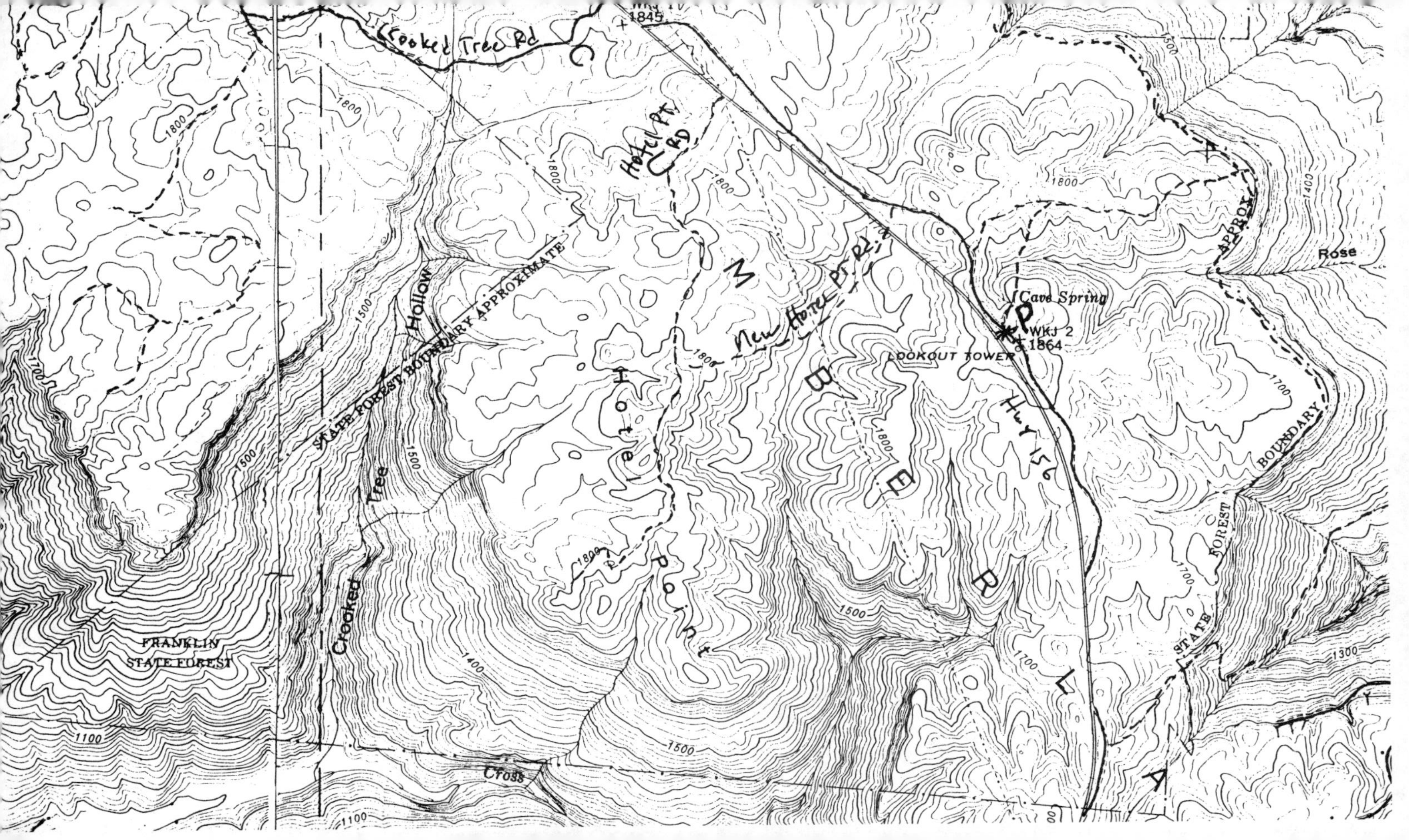

Crooked Tree Rd
C
Hotel Pt Rd
M
New Hotel Pt Rd
B
E
R
L
A
Hwy 156
Cave Spring
WKJ 2
1864
LOOKOUT TOWER
Rose
APPROX
STATE FOREST BOUNDARY
Hotel Point
Hollow
Crooked Tree
STATE FOREST BOUNDARY APPROXIMATE
FRANKLIN STATE FOREST
Cross
1845

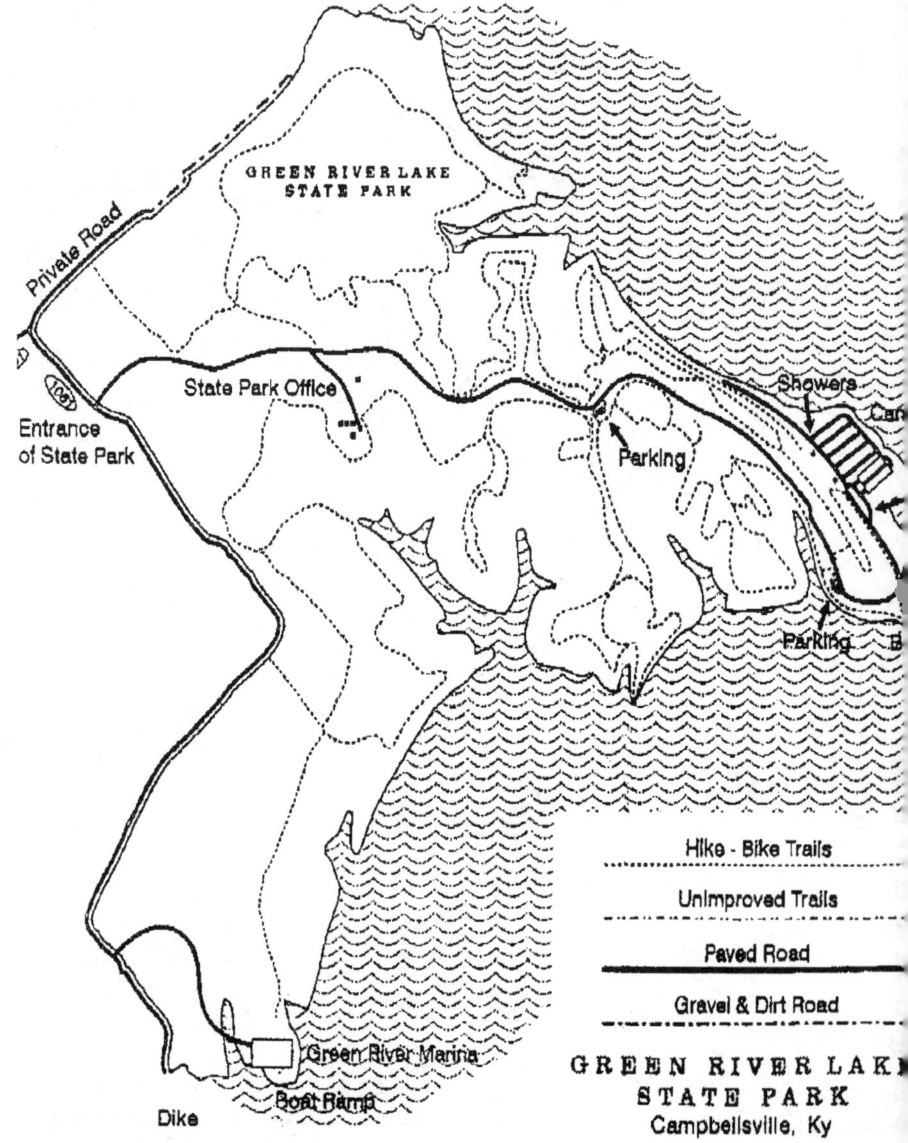
GREEN RIVER LAKE
STATE PARK
Private Road
1061
Entrance
of State Park
State Park Office
Parking
Showers
Parking
Green River Marina
Boat Ramp
Dike
Hike - Bike Trails
Unimproved Trails
Paved Road
Gravel & Dirt Road
GREEN RIVER LAK
STATE PARK
Campbellsville, Ky

GREEN RIVER STATE PARK, KY

Although it's not it Tennessee, you need to check this place out. It was built exclusively by a group of mountain bikers and it shows. Talk about an excellent network of trails. You can ride all day, on all types of terrain. The area is consistent with the Cumberland Plateau, lots of rolling hills with several big valleys thrown in.

You will not find a specific loop or a one-way trail. They have constructed more than 15 miles of trails that offer endless loops. If you want an easy ride you have the option to stay on most of the ridges through bypasses. Our wives rode on top while we dropped into the valleys and climbed out to meet back up with them.

The south side of the park is bordered by the lake and it is beautiful. There is one area you ride into that would make an excellent camp. Take a minute here for a quick swim, it will give you something to look back on as you climb back to the top of the ridge.

The trails on the north side were constructed in '95 and '96 and some of them were still rough when we rode there. This is the extreme part of the park. There are some really steep gorges that are climbable with good conditions and strong legs. If you get caught up in the clay/sand, keep going and it will end eventually.

As a State Park there are other things to do. It boasts a large campground, bathrooms and a playground. I was surprised with all the beauty of the mountain bike trails with hills and trees to have the campground on a flat rocky shoreline. Take your tent and get into the back country if you plan to camp.

Directions. Green River State Park is located just south of Campbellsville, Ky. Exit off the Cumberland Parkway and drive north on Hwy. 55. Continue north for several miles until you reach Hwy. 1061. This is a right turn to the park. There will be a State Park sign on the corner. It is not easy to reach, but the riding is worth the drive.

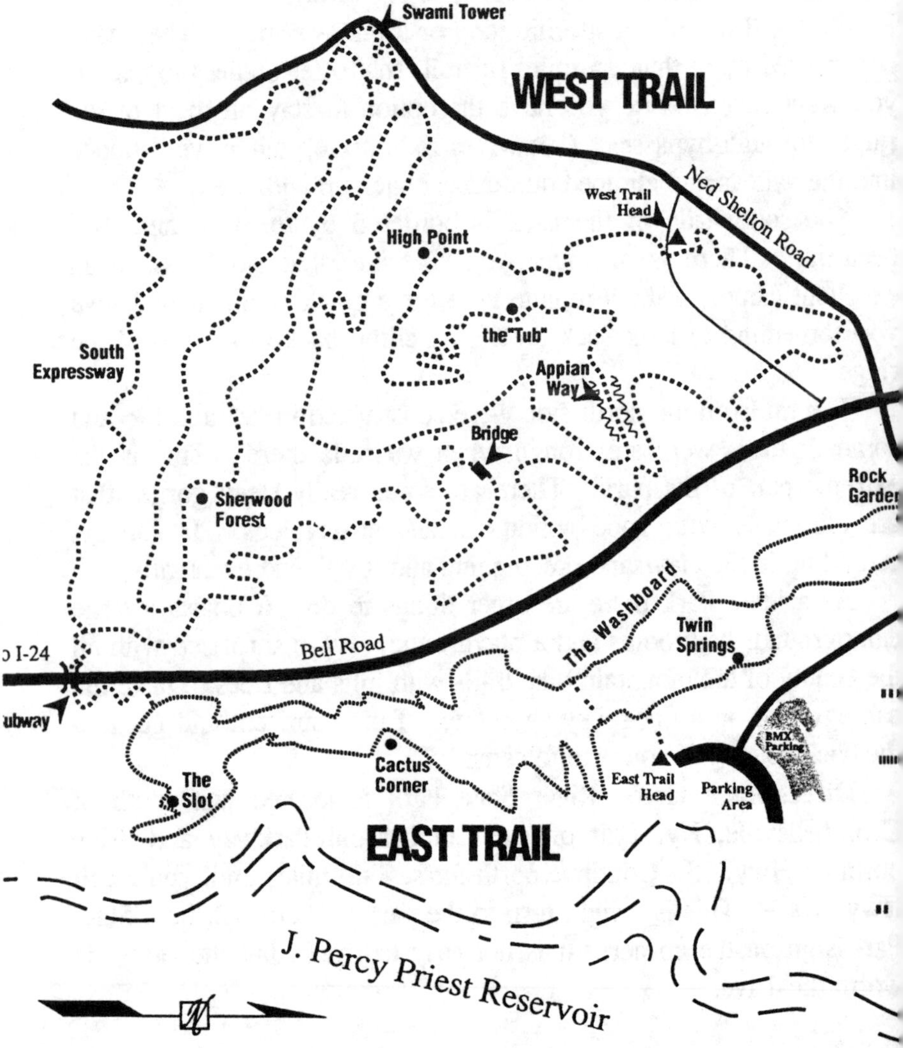

Swami Tower

WEST TRAIL

Ned Shelton Road

West Trail Head

High Point

the "Tub"

South Expressway

Appian Way

Bridge

Sherwood Forest

Rock Garden

The Washboard

Twin Springs

Bell Road

o I-24

ubway

BMX Parking

The Slot

Cactus Corner

East Trail Head

Parking Area

EAST TRAIL

J. Percy Priest Reservoir

For More Informati

HAMILTON CREEK

Nashville's newest mountain bike area has opened and made a lot of locals happy. Designed to replace Percy Warner, it lacks the hills, but makes up for it with challenging singletrack. Currently there are 11 miles of trails. With riding suitable for all levels of expertise, we now have a viable option for off-road riding locally.

Hamilton Creek is divided by Bell Road. The East trail, running along Percy Priest Lake, is designed as a beginner and intermediate area. This three-mile loop offers scenic yet fairly demanding riding for riders wanting an off-road experience in a limited capacity.

The West trail consists of seven miles of more challenging single track. This is an advanced area that offers rocks, roots, logs, ledges, hill climbs, and switch backs. First-time riders and beginners should stay on the East trail. To eliminate possible conflicts with drivers on Bell Road, we have access to a culvert which passes under the road. We must use caution and walk our bikes through here. Be aware: Two-way traffic can be encountered at any time. Both trails are fun to ride in either direction. Each way has different challenges.

All I can say is if you live in Middle Tennessee or are visiting, come out and try Hamilton Creek. It's fun, challenging riding that will improve your skills. If you like a workout, Hamilton Creek delivers. A special thanks to a handful of Mountain Trails members who made this happen: Tommy, Stephen, Paul, Bo and many others including the Metro Parks and Recreation Department.

Directions: Take I-40 east from Nashville, exit on Stewart's Ferry Pike and go south. Continue past Elm Hill Marina and Recreation Area until you see the Hamilton Creek sign. Turn left at the entrance, then take the first right. Follow this road to your right towards the south end. This is where the trail head begins.

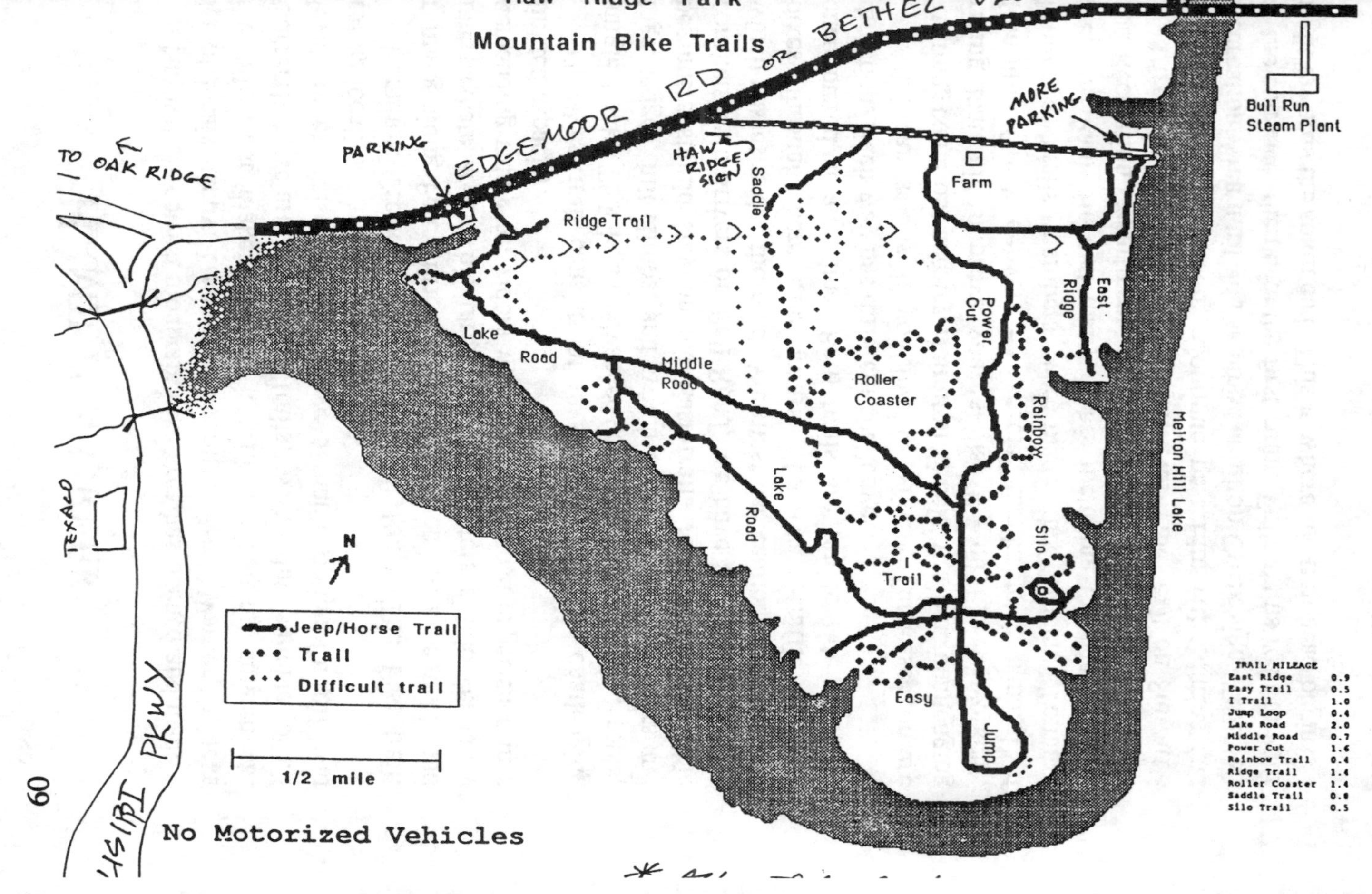

Haw Ridge Park
Mountain Bike Trails
TO OAK RIDGE
PARKING
EDGEMOOR RD OR BETHEL
HAW RIDGE SIGN
MORE PARKING
Bull Run Steam Plant
Farm
Ridge Trail
Saddle
Lake Road
Middle Road
Roller Coaster
Power Cut
Ridge
East
Rainbow
Melton Hill Lake
Lake Road
Silo
I Trail
Easy
Jump
TEXACO
N
Jeep/Horse Trail
Trail
Difficult trail
1/2 mile
PKWY
No Motorized Vehicles
TRAIL MILEAGE
East Ridge 0.9
Easy Trail 0.5
I Trail 1.0
Jump Loop 0.4
Lake Road 2.0
Middle Road 0.7
Power Cut 1.6
Rainbow Trail 0.4
Ridge Trail 1.4
Roller Coaster 1.4
Saddle Trail 0.8
Silo Trail 0.5

HAW RIDGE PARK

Located just outside of Oak Ridge, Haw Ridge is a long-time favorite place to ride for Knoxvillians. With 700 acres of hilly lakefront terrain, riders can find nearly any type of trail they want. If you like it steep, ride Ridge Trail from the west to get your thighs burning, then follow the Saddle over to Roller Coaster. Like jeep roads? They too have some steep sections but several nice loops can be pieced together without hitting the extreme trails. Just feel like exploring? With 12 miles of trails, you can go in many directions and never get lost.

Riders of all abilities will find trails they like here, from Power Cut and Lake Road for the beginner or intermediate to the steeps of Ridge Trail for advanced riders. Trails consist of dirt jeep roads (some are quite rocky) and single track throughout the woods. Most riders park at the west entrance. Regardless of where you start, there is a good climb waiting to get you warmed up.

There may be some changes coming in future years as the city is working to develop a "master plan" for the park. Eventually a full scale development could take place.

Directions: Going north on Pellisippi Pkwy., turn right as soon as you cross the river on Edgemoor Rd. (Bethel Valley). Park in the gravel area along the road or follow the road to the right into the park.

LOST OR STOLEN

Write your name, address, phone number and *This Bike is Stolen* on a piece of masking tape and stick it to the fork's steer tube or inside your seat post. Then if your bike is ever stolen, someday a shop mechanic may contact you in the middle of a repair and make your day.

HERB PARSONS LAKE

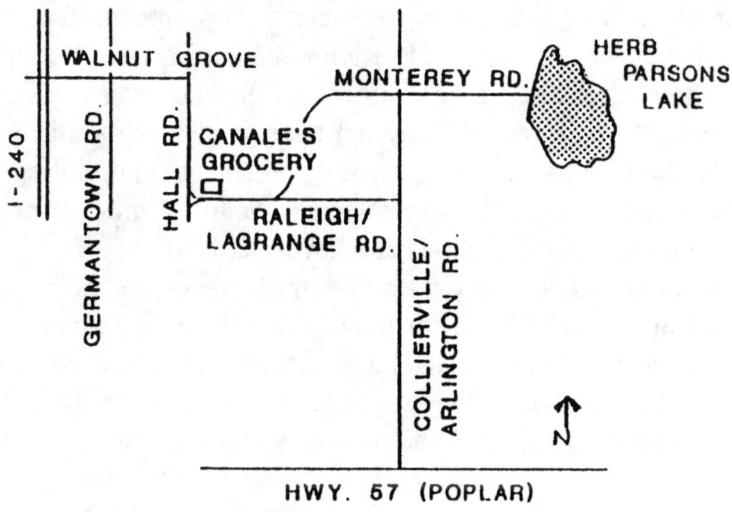

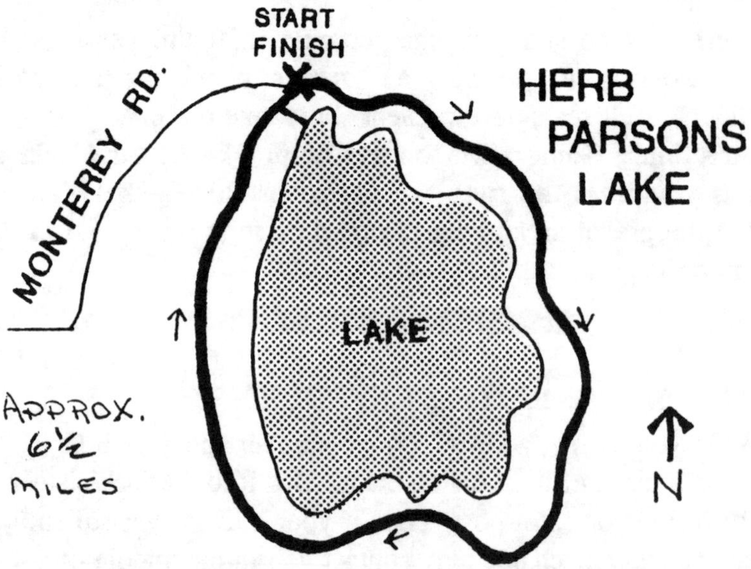

HERB PARSONS STATE PARK

Herb Parsons State Park is one of the few State Parks in Tennessee currently allowing mountain bikers to use their trails. We have made great progress at opening up new Parks. Let's hope it continues. This has been an outstanding riding area for Memphis riders.

You will find approximately seven miles of trails that run along the shoreline. There are several technical areas that involve frequent tree crossings and very tight singletrack. You should also beware of wet areas and walk your bike when necessary. The soil in West Tennessee is much more conducive to rutting than the rest of the state, so it is important to give some riding time back to the trails in the form of work days. The long-term ramifications pay big dividends.

There are additional trails planned for the summer of '97 running along higher terrain. This should allow for some riding while the original trail is too soft. Again, these trails are being constructed by local cyclists in conjunction with park officials. For those of you looking for additional trails, most of our new access is in direct relation to our construction abilities. Park your bike for awhile and pull some maintenance or help the dedicated that continue to increase our trail networks. Good going guys!

Herb Parsons has been host to several fat tire races, I hope we will see more races and mountain bike events here in the future. One of the rangers asks that you not park behind the gates if you plan to ride past dark.

Directions: From I-40, take St. Route 205 south to Fisherville. At the intersection of St. Route 193 turn left and follow the signs to Herb Parsons State Park. The trail follows the levee entering the woods on the south end of the lake.

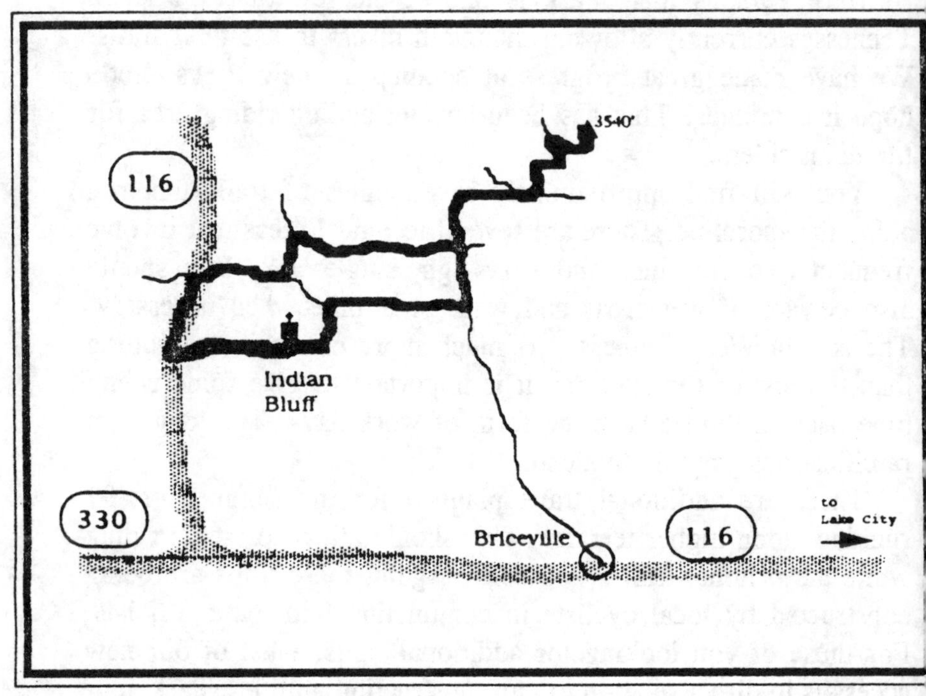
3540'
116
Indian
Bluff
330
to
Lake City
Briceville
116

INDIAN BLUFF LOOP

Located north of Knoxville is a challenging ride that will take you to some of the highest terrain west of the Appalachians, climbing to over 3,500 feet. I have not had the opportunity to explore this ride yet. The following information was provided by an anonymous adventurer of the Appalachian Mountain Bike Club.

Description: Starting at the end of the pavement of Braden Flats Road (1,940'), the trail forks in less than .1 mile. Take the left fork and climb steeply under a power line until you reach a junction at a coal seam (mile .6, 2,340'). Turn right (east) and follow the coal seam to its intersection (mile 2.8, 2,160') with the gravel road from Briceville. (Briceville is 3.1 miles down the road to the right) Turn left and begin the 3.1-mile climb to Cross Mountain, the highest point east of the Rockies and west of the Appalachians. At mile 3.6 (2,700) notice the road to the left – you will be turning there on your way back. At mile 4.4 you arrive at Grassy Gap (3,000'), with views of the Tennessee Valley to the east and the Cumberland Mountains to the west. A gravel road to the left descends to coal seams but continues north to a dirt road on the left at mile 4.7. Follow this dirt road to mile 5.7 and take the sharp right up to the radio towers (mile 5.9, 3,540'). Pavement and building structures remain from a 1950s radar station. Return on the same route to mile 8 (2,700'), where you take a right along another coal seam. At mile 10.3 (2,800'), take the dirt road descending south. At mile 10.9 (2,340') you intersect the lower coal seam. Continue right (southwest) to Graves Gap (mile 11.3, 2,160') on highway 116. Turn left down 116 to Braden Flats Road (mile 11.8).

The total distance for this ride is 13.1 miles, and it should be considered a moderate to strenuous three-hour ride. Once again, many thanks to the unknown rider who discovered this loop.

Directions: Park near the Indian Bluff Baptist Church on Braden Flats Road, about three miles north of the junction of 330 and 116 west of Lake City.

LAND BETWEEN THE LAKES

The Tennessee Valley Authority's 170,000-acre Land Between the Lakes in western Kentucky and Tennessee offers excellent mountain biking opportunities. T.V.A. is doing some experimenting with us and has recently opened part of their North-South hiking trail to assess user conflicts and the impact of mountain bikes. This is a one-year experiment, so it's up to us to make a good impression. As of the writing of this update, we are allowed access to the trail via the Jenny Ridge Trail. This is great news because the N/S trail is a single-track rider's dream. The trail is well marked and offers a variety of terrain. If you are the type of rider that likes to explore, give LBL a try.

The Jenny Ridge trail is 12 miles long, most of which is singletrack along the North/South trail. Riding here is not only beautiful with all the views of the lake, it's a blast. The trails are a lot like Tsali: you ride in and out along the coves of Kentucky Lake. Bald Eagles are flying overhead, fish are jumping and you're supposed to concentrate on a little trail. Even better is the terrain. There are many excellent climbs and most end with fun, fast descents along tight tree-strewn ridges. I really get excited about riding here. Even though it's hilly, most riders can climb the hills (although some are pretty long). The great thing is by riding the whole trail it's a 25-mile day of great riding. You can park at the Golden Pond Visitor's Center or the Jenny Ridge Picnic Area and access the trail from either. Look for it on the west side of the parkway.

Many of the access trails were built by PAMBA, a mountain bike club out of Paducah. They are the ones keeping this place so sweet. Make sure you fill out a visitor's card at the welcome center to let them know how much you like riding here. As of this writing, park officials are planning to re-open the trails north of Sugar Bay for riding. The trails were closed during the winter due to trail damage. This additional access to the North / South trail is some of the finest riding available. If they are closed when you go, stay off. LBL is discussing a user fee for access to these and other trails, pay them graciously. It is a small price to pay.

When you visit L.B.L., don't limit yourself just to these trails. There are many miles of old dirt jeep roads here, and accurate maps are available at the Visitor's Center. Please use common sense when riding here and eventually we may have access to 50-60 miles of hiking trails.

Directions: From Nashville, take I-24 east into Kentucky. Exit on Hwy 68 and follow the signs to the Land Between the Lakes. Exit at Golden Pond, this will put you on "The Trace". Turn right, the visitors center is on the right with restrooms and additional information. As you continue north a couple hundred yards, there is a wide gravel shoulder, the top of the Jenny Ridge trail leads to the left here. The Jenny Ridge parking area is another half mile down the road, you can also pick the trail up there. Drive time from Nashville is about two and a half hours.

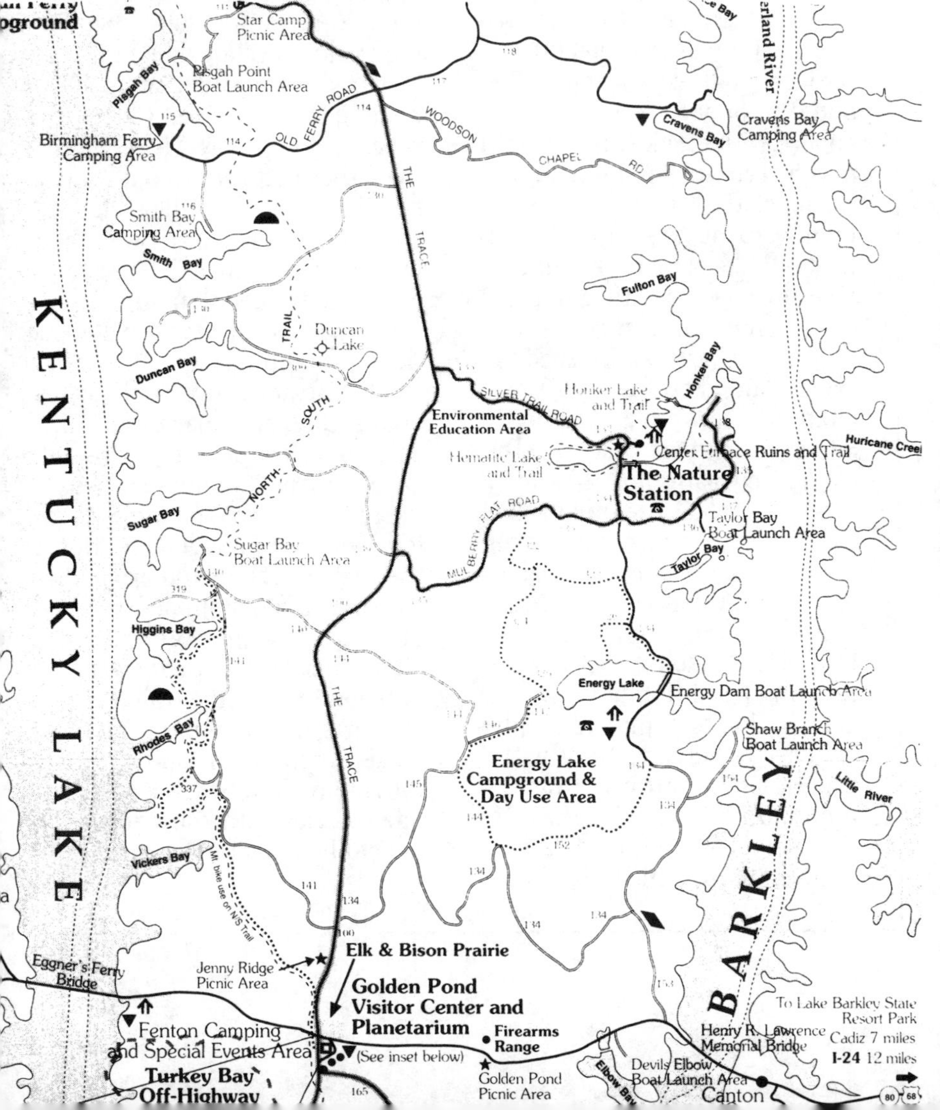

LONG HUNTER TO REMAIN CLOSED

Mike Cole, park manager at Long Hunter State Park, says that the Bryant Grove Trail will remain closed to mountain bikes until further notice. He regrets this decision, but maintains that his first responsibility is to protect the resources of the park and his second is to provide recreational opportunities. Mike says the trail may be reopened to bikes in the spring of 1998 if planned trail improvements are completed next winter. Mike closed the trail to bikes in November 1996 to prevent use when it is muddy.

Citations are being issued to cyclists found on the trail. The citation is $2, with an additional $98 in court costs. Mike said they are actively patrolling the trail heads, as well as the trail itself via the park's radio-linked mountain bike and all-terrain utility vehicle.

"I regret that we've had to close this trail to bikes," Mike told MTBC, adding that it would remain closed to bikes until the park is able to complete its plan to "pave" muddy sections with gravel. He is optimistic that mountain biking will return to the park at some future date.

Even though the trail will be dry for most of the summer, Mike says he won't reopen it because some cyclists ignored his signs when he closed the trail during wet weather, adding that it takes too much time for his staff to baby-sit the trail for cycling. Mike told us he witnessed a parent and child reading the "Trail Wet, Closed to Bikes" sign one day. The child told the father that they weren't supposed to ride. The father told the child they would go anyway. Mike, who in disbelief had listened to this exchange from within an unmarked patrol car, then stopped them for a little talk.

The Bryant Grove Trail has several features that make it unsuitable for year-round bicycle use. It crosses many low areas close to Percy Priest Lake and often floods, leaving it wet for a good portion of the year. To compound problems, the trail suffers from poor drainage, leaving water in the trail after rains. MTBC supports his decision to close the trail and is encouraged that he is trying to make the trail more suitable for mountain biking. Please let everyone you ride with know about this hopefully temporary closure.

LONG HUNTER STAT PARK

Long Hunter is one of the newest areas ... mountain biking. Currently we are only ... th Bryant Grove Trail, a scenic four-mile ... Perc Priest Lake. An out-and-back trip is eig ... .celler ride for all abilities. Most of the trail is ... in som sections. It is wide enough in most ... technic skills are not essential.

If you are interested in a ... e where yo can bring your family, this ... tant factor t keep in mind: We are in ... e. The one rul you must abide by is *not* ... five days after rains. This soil does nc ... e was a significar amount of damage dc ... period of time. Th rangers have tried t ... the wet trails, but few people have d ... v all loose access t this park for ridin ... ride here if it ha rained recently. As o ... four articles in th *Tennessean* about ride ... the trails are poste closed. This does nc ... when seeking access t additional State Par ... ır friends, closed mear closed.

Directions: I ... k is 10 miles south of M Juliet on Mt. Ju ... trail head, turn left into th park entrance ... office. Take the first left an follow it to ... to the right. To check and se if the trails ... ffice at 615-885-2422.

CLOSED!

This can happen to your favorite trail too.
Join your local mountain bike club today - Get involved - Be pro-active - If you don't play by the rules, we all loose.

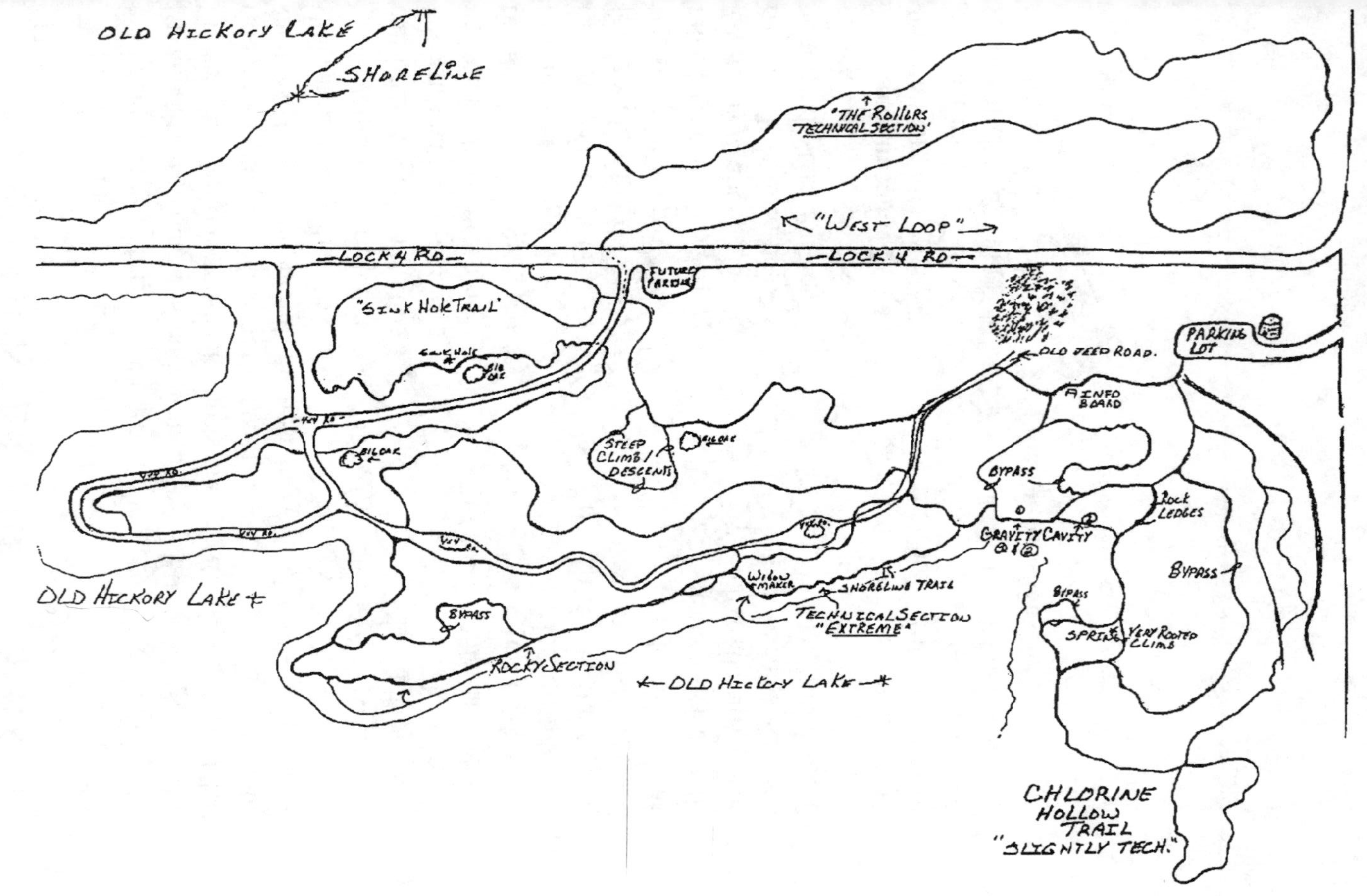
OLD HICKORY LAKE
SHORELINE
"THE Rollers
TECHNICAL SECTION"
"WEST LOOP"
LOCK 4 RD
LOCK 4 RD
FUTURE PARKING
"SINK HOLE TRAIL"
OLD JEEP ROAD.
PARKING LOT
INFO BOARD
STEEP CLIMB / DESCENTS
BYPASS
ROCK LEDGES
GRAVITY CAVITY
① & ②
BYPASS
WIDOW MAKER
SHORELINE TRAIL
TECHNICAL SECTION
"EXTREME"
BYPASS
SPRING
VERY ROOTED CLIMB
OLD HICKORY LAKE
BYPASS
ROCKY SECTION
OLD HICKORY LAKE
CHLORINE HOLLOW TRAIL
"SLIGHTLY TECH."

LOCK 4

This is the pride and joy of the Sumner County Cycling Club, our backyard playground. We have taken the best of Sumner County and built a mountain bike trail around it. Among the rolling hills around Old Hickory Lake we've carved out five miles of good clean fun. Consisting of mostly single track, you'll climb and descend through several valleys, ride a rocky trail along the lake and switch back among the cedar trees. All in all, you'll get a good workout. We've built by-passes around the most technical areas so everyone can enjoy riding here. Special thanks to my friends Sam, Les, Jan, Sara, Jerry, Tommy and all the others who built these trails and work continously to ensure their upkeep.

Directions: From Nashville, take I-65 N to Vietnam Veterans Blvd. Follow east as the bypass runs into Gallatin Road, go 2.5 miles past Volunteer State Community College. At the fourth light, turn right on Lock 4 Road. Follow this all the way to the end (four miles). As you enter the park, look for the silo. This is the parking area. The trails leave from the corner of the parking lot.

HELPFUL HINTS

Recommended tools to carry while riding:

1. A chain tool compatible with your chain.
2. A patch kit or spare tube. I recommend a patch kit since you can get more than one flat.
3. A tire pump. CO_2 is fast, but how many will you need?
4. Tire levers. Kevlar bead tires are extremely hard to get off. If you don't have levers, try the quick release from your hubs.
5. Tuck an extra Powerbar in your bag. I've been on many two-hour trips that turned into four.
6. Iodine tablets to purify water in case you run out.
7. Tools such as allen wrenches, screwdrivers, etc. There are some very nice tool kits available.

These are not luxuries, they're necessities.

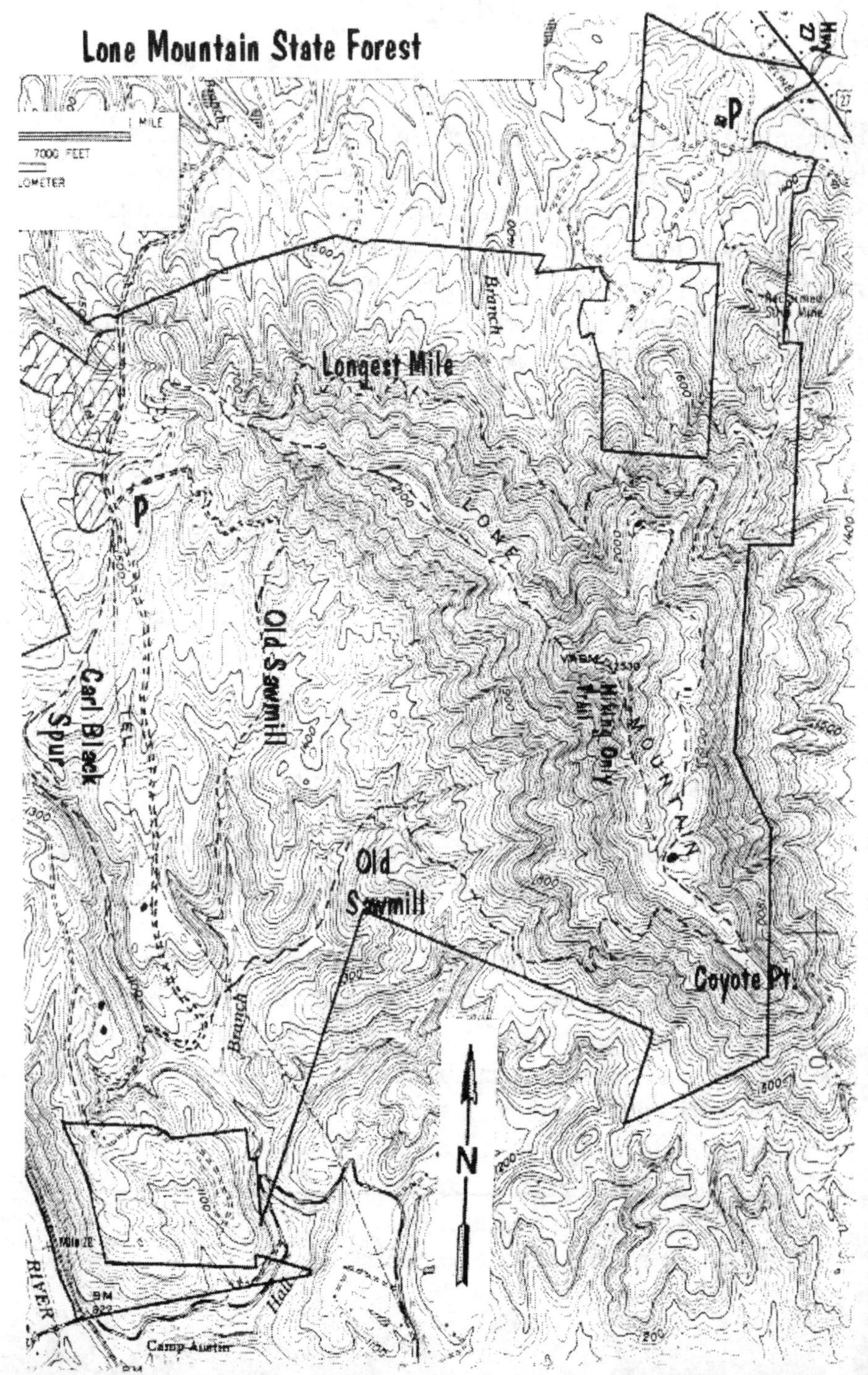
Lone Mountain State Forest
MILE
7000 FEET
Longest Mile
Branch
P
P
LONE
MOUNTAIN
Old Sawmill
Carl Black
Spur
Hiking Only Trail
Old
Sawmill
Coyote Pt.
Branch
N
RIVER
Camp Austin
Hwy 27

LONE MOUNTAIN

The first time I rode here I vowed to keep it secret for my special riding place. Lone Mountain has everything I love about mountain biking: long, steep, never-ending hill climbs; steep, technical and long descents; always another beautiful view around each corner, and trails well suited for riding. When I am out for a tough ride, Lone Mountain is at the top of my list.

You can start from the Rangers Station or at The Longest Mile. Either way you are going to do a lot of climbing. From the Rangers Station the road is rideable except for one spot. Once you reach The Longest Mile trail, the worst is over. Ride up to Coyote Point for a beautiful overlook, then payback time as you descend down Old Sawmill. Plan to take this to The Longest Mile. The Carl Black Spur is rough and rocky. It is a good option if you want to make an even more difficult loop. Starting at The Longest Mile, you're still going to be climbing but the scenery is outstanding. You work your way up the mountain in and out of drainage's, each offering a great view down below. Once you reach the junction on top, turn right out to Coyote Point and then hang on for a fast, rocky, technical downhill. Stay straight to reach the Carl Black Spur, another tough trail, or turn right and follow Old Sawmill for a shorter route back to the trailhead.

Keep in mind these are horse trails and use common sense. The hiking trail is off limits! Stop in and say hi to the rangers. They don't mind us riding let's keep it that way.

Directions: Located just off Hwy. 27, three miles south of Wartburg. There is a convenience store (Quality Oil) at the turnoff. Turn left on Clayton Howard Road, and the park office and parking area are 3/4 of a mile on the right. Park in the parking area at the trail head. There is a new parking area where the Longest Mile joins Carl Black Spur. The main trail down to the Forestry Office has gotten pretty rutted, so you may want to by-pass it. Maps are available in the office. For information, Brant Miller, 423-346-6655.

THE TRAIL STARTS HERE...

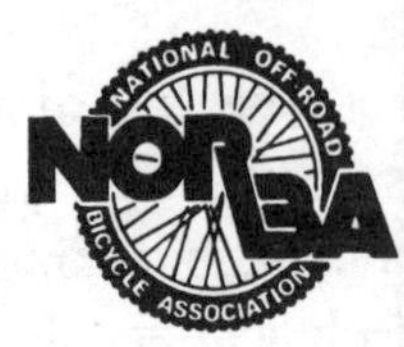

MEMBERSHIP APPLICATION

1. RIDER INFORMATION:

Name______________________________

Residential Address________________________

City__________ State________ Zip______

Phone ( ) ________________

2. BIRTHDATE:

Month________ Day________ Year________

3. SEX:

☐ Female ☐ Male

4. U.S. CITIZEN?

☐ Yes ☐ No

5. CLASS: (Age as of 12/31/93)

☐ Junior 12-18 yrs.
☐ Senior 19-34 yrs.
☐ Veteran 35-44 yrs.
☐ Master 45+

6. CATEGORY

CROSS COUNTRY
☐ Beginner - New competitor
☐ Sport - Intermediate competitor
☐ Expert - Advanced competitor
☐ Pro/Elite - Requires upgrade

DOWNHILL
☐ Beginner - New competitor
☐ Sport - Intermediate competitor
☐ Expert - Advanced competitor
☐ Pro/Elite - Requires upgrade

OBSERVED TRIALS
☐ Beginner - New competitor
☐ Sport - Intermediate competitor
☐ Pro/Expert - Requires upgrade

7. MEMBERSHIP STATUS

☐ New Member
☐ Renewal Lic. #__________

8. FEES

☐ Annual license: $25
☐ 2-year license: $45 (Available for new members only)
☐ Current USCF Member Lic. # __________ : $15
☐ Donation to support national land access efforts for mountain bikers:
☐ $5 ☐ $10 ☐ $20 ☐ Other
☐ Donation to support U.S. World Championship Team:
☐ $5 ☐ $10 ☐ $20 ☐ Other

Total payment enclosed: $________________

Payment:
☐ Check ☐ Money order

☐ Visa ☐ Mastercard

Cardholder name:________________

Credit card#:________________

Credit card expiration date:________________

Cardholder signature:________________

AGREEMENT AND RELEASE OF LIABILITY
(With consent of parent or guardian of minor)

I am an amateur in good standing and wish to be a licensed athlete under the Racing Rules of the National Off-Road Bicycle Association (NORBA). I certify that the information on this application, as entered by me, is true and correct.

I acknowledge that cycling is an inherently dangerous sport in which I participate at my own risk and that NORBA is a non-profit corporation formed to advance the sport of cycling, the efforts of which directly benefit me. In consideration of the agreement of NORBA to issue an amateur license to me, hereby on behalf of myself, my heirs, assigns and personal representatives, i release and forever discharge NORBA and the United States Cycling Federation, Its employees, agents, members, sponsors, promoters, and waive any such claims against any such person or organization, arising directly or indirectly from or attributable to in any legal way to any action or omission to act of any such person or organization in connection with sponsorship, organization or execution of any bicycle racing or sporting event, including travel to and from such an event, in which I may participate as a rider, team member or spectator.

I currently have no known physical or mental condition that would impair capability for full participation as intended and expected or me (except for).

____
Signature of Applicant Date

PARENT OR GUARDIAN OF MINOR (Under age 18): I, as parent or guardian of applicant, represent to NORBA that the facts herein concerning my child or ward true. I hereby give my permission for my child or ward to enter any bicycle race event for which a permit has been issued by NORBA during the period of the lice applied for, and further, in consideration of granting such license, agree, indivi ally and on behalf of my child or ward, to the terms of the above Agreement Release of Liability

____
Signature or Parent or Guardian Date

Send application & check or money order payable to NORBA to: (Allow 30 days to receive your license.)

NORBA LICENSE DES
ONE OLYMPIC PLAZA, COLORADO SPRINGS, CO 80909 • (719) 578-47

MONTEREY

The Cumberland Plateau has held my interest for many years, but I was not able to find the trails to ride. I have had a contact in Cookeville, but until recently we never had the opportunity to ride together. Well, Wayne, Mark, Josh and a bunch of friends finally hooked up, and now you're going to benefit from it.

Located just minutes from I-40, are four and ten mile rides that intermediate riders will enjoy. The four miler is a fast four-wheeler trail. Riding along then down one hillside, you splash through a creek and begin the climb back up. You can ride in either direction. Clockwise provides the longest downhill and steepest climb. Counterclockwise offers a fast ride with some sharp corners. Make sure you follow the trail to the left when riding this way. The right trail leads you on the 10-mile loop.

The 10-miler is a lot tougher. You will ride along and under the power lines, which offers some huge climbs. Make sure you bring some extra water on this ride. You'll want it. The four-wheeler trails lead you in and out of the woods, eventually bringing you home. There are many additional jeep roads to explore from this parking area. They are uncharted so check your surroundings.

Directions: On I-40 get off on Monterey exit #301. Turn south (away from town) and follow this road for about 1 to 1.5 miles, turn left on Hillwood Street. Park on the gravel road 50 yards up on the right, or under the power lines. The trailhead leads clockwise by following the trail leading into the woods to the left under the power lines by the road. You can follow the jeep trail along Hillwood Street and when you cross Hwy. 70, you can actually make you way to Monteray Lake by way of jeep trails. This is another huge network of trails, take some time and explore.

For more information about local rides or to get supplies, call Bill at Smith's Bike Shop in Cookeville at 615-528-7848 or Cookeville Bicycle Shop at 520-6161.

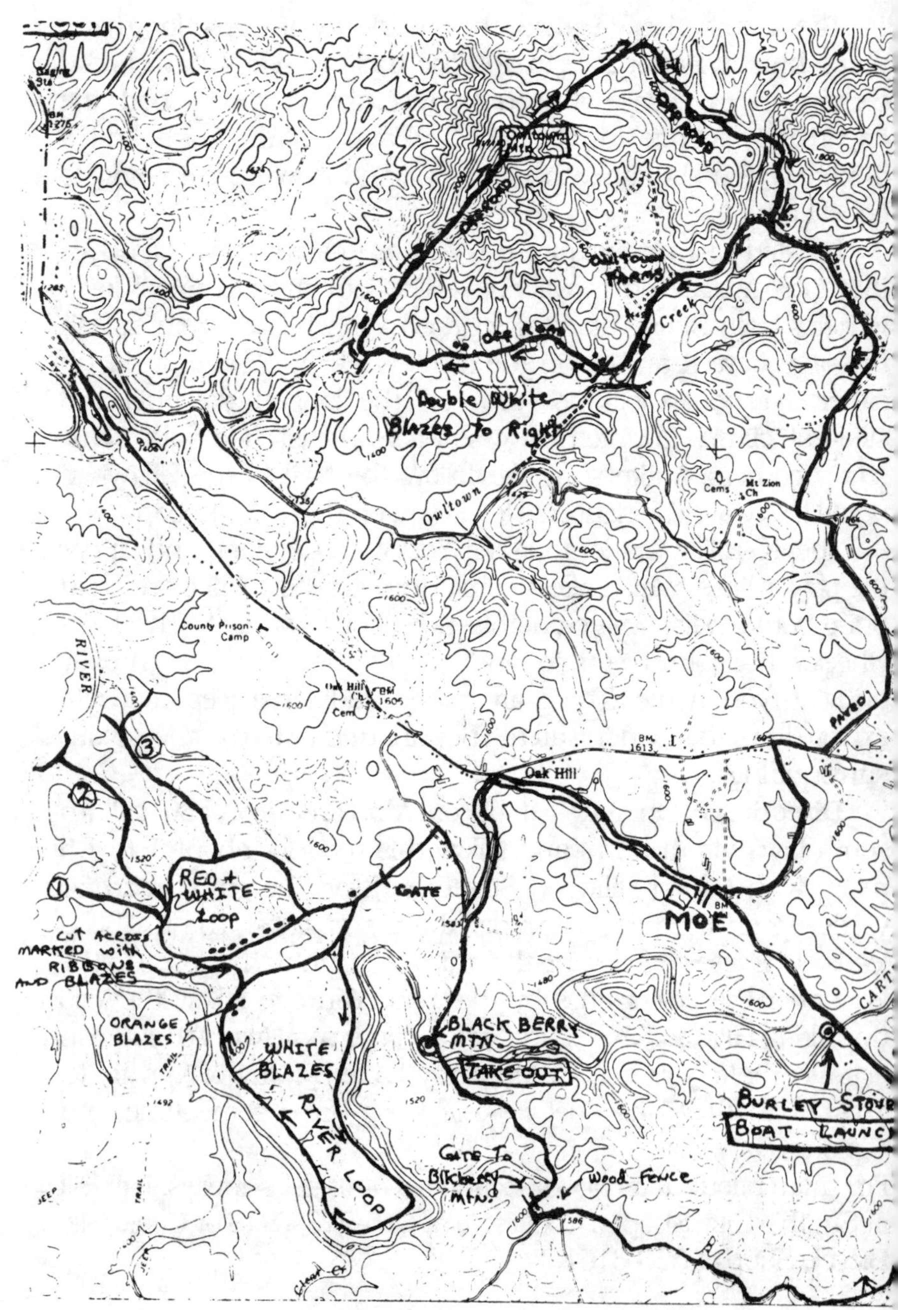
Owltown Mtn
Owltown Farms
Creek
Double White
Blazes to Right
Owltown
Cems
Mt Zion Ch
County Prison Camp
RIVER
Oak Hill Ch
Cem
BM 1605
BM 1613
Oak Hill
PAVED
RED + WHITE Loop
GATE
MOE
CUT ACROSS MARKED with RIBBONS AND BLAZES
ORANGE BLAZES
WHITE BLAZES
RIVER LOOP
BLACK BERRY MTN
TAKE OUT
GATE TO Blkberry MTN.
Wood Fence
BURLEY STOVE
BOAT LAUNCH
TRAIL
JEEP

M.O.E.

Mountaintown Outdoor Expeditions is located in the heart of the Chattahoochee National Forest and is home to one of the most popular destinations for mountain bikers in the Southeast. Six miles east of Ellijay on Hwy. 52 you'll find the 18-bunk MOEtel and two tough, technical trails.

Owltown Loop is an 11-miler with an infamous 800-foot vertical climb which is rumored to make even the experts carry their bikes. The River Loop drops down the mountain to the Cartecay River, then snakes its way home. This six-mile loop is rough and tough. There is also a connector to the Red and White Loop. I suggest some side trips to the river.

While you're there, check out the **Rich Mountain Trail**. This was the toughest ride we found, with 1,200' climbs and steep drop-offs, this is one thrilling 8 mile trail. The trail ends at Deep Gap at Aska Rd. If you want more, there are three more miles across the road. This climbs Green Mtn. for a scenic overlook of Lake Blue Ridge. Then the trail descends to the shores of the lake. You can backtrack on the trail or loop around Campbell Camp Road and connect back to Aska Rd. Then choose a road ride or the singletrack back to the parking area. The climbs are steep and rocky, the descents non-ending and out of this world. I have the scars to prove it. Intermediate riders will probably not enjoy the extreme nature of Rich Mtn. but if you are looking for a challenging ride with screaming, tight downhills, make the climb.

Directions. From Blue Ridge, south on E. First St. 1.1 mi. to GA Hwy. 515. Drive south 6.1 miles to crossing of Rock Creek, turn right. Follow Rock Creek Rd. East, the pavement will end in 1.8 mi.. The parking area is the Checking station in 2.2 miles. There is limited parking on top of the mountain another mile up the road. It's at least an hour from Bear Creek.

For more info: MOE, Ellijay, GA, 706-635-2524, or call the Toccoa Ranger District in Blue Ridge. 404-632-3031.

RIGHT NOW, THERE'S A GUY WITH A ROUTER CARVING A WOODEN SIGN THAT WILL UNCEREMONI BE POSTED AT A TRAILHEAD SOMEWHERE. It's a simple sign. And very easy to comprehend: No bikes.

Perhaps even more disturbing is the fact that this sign is not limited to just a handful of trails in just a handful of areas around the country.

From Marin to Moab to New Hampshire, trail access to mountain bikes is being threatened at an alarming rate. One estimate has one trail closing for every single day of the year. And up on Mount Tamalpais, the birthplace of mountain biking, it's no big secret that park rangers, armed with radar guns, lie in ambush hoping to "discourage" cyclists with $200 speeding tickets.

So how did this happen? How did a sport that started innocently enough on a couple of fat tire bikes end up the target for the biggest quarantine since smallpox? And more importantly, who's responsible?

Oops, there go all the fingers. Hikers pointing at bikers. Bikers pointing at equestrians. And isn't it funny, no one is pointing at themselves. Maybe that's the problem. Maybe we as mountain bikers need to take a long hard look at ourselves.

Hikers will tell you they've been around forever and that they've paid their dues by helping secure land, by building and maintaining trails and
cating the public to help insure a more respectful wil
experience. And who can argue? After all, most of us
trails the hikers and equestrians helped establish. Bu
if anything, are we
uting in return? C
there are mounta
clubs and groups
for land access b
many of us are
involved? How ma
know there's a prob
there? How man
even care?

TRAIL CLOSED

CHECKPOINT : REALITY

We're not sug
that everyone jum
bandwagon nor
suggesting that ev
who rides a mountain bike become a martyr for th
We're merely suggesting that, as cyclists, we need
becoming more aware of what's going on; that we're
only ones on the trail and that, when it comes to land
there are a lot of legitimate gripes con
everyone involved—not just bikers.

There is no simple solution to any of
maybe, just maybe, by first trying to und
the various points of view out there we
start to get a handle on this thing.

Meanwhile the guy with the router
orders as fast as he can.

FIND OUT WHERE EVERYONE'S AT ON THE TRAIL:

International Mountain Bicycling Association
(IMBA)
PO Box 412043
Los Angeles, CA 90041
(818) 792-8830

American Hiking Society
(AHS)
PO Box 20160
Washington, D.C. 20041-2160
(703) 385-3252

American Horse Council
(AHC)
[illegible]
Washington, D.C. [illegible]
(202) 296-4031
Contact: Amy Mann

Brought to you as a public service by Specialized and this publication.

NATCHEZ TRACE STATE PARK

Traveling west on I-40 you'll find a mountain biker's paradise. Natchez Trace is both a State Park and Wildlife Management Area. It seems the entire 45,000 acres were designed with the recreational user in mind.

First of all, the rangers are happy to have us riding in their park. Stay off the hiking trails—some riders have been fined. More importantly, you'll find more than 100 miles of trails legal to ride on that are generally well marked and in pretty good condition. These access roads, horse trails, and fire roads vary from packed gravel roads to old dirt paths.

Interested in beautiful scenery? This place has it. Most of West Tennessee is flat; Natchez Trace is not. The hills are consistently rolling, with elevation gains of 100 to 200 feet. Most of the hills are rideable, but you're sure to get a good workout.

I would rate most of the trails acceptable for beginning riders as well as more advanced riders. The beginners will find well-marked trails in good condition while more advanced riders will have the opportunity to ride some fairly challenging terrain for endless miles. The best trails are located on the north and west sides of the park.

This is a Wildlife Management Area so you can expect to see a wide variety of wildlife including turkey, coyote, deer, fox, and many others. Keep in mind that hunters are welcome here. I'd stay away during hunting season.

If you would like to spend the night, camping is available and there is a nice lodge. There is a restaurant on site and plenty of activities for the spouse and kids if they don't want to ride.

Directions: Natchez Trace State Park is located approximately one and a half hours west of Nashville and east of Memphis. Take I-40 to the Natchez Trace exit, turn south and follow this road to the Visitor's Center on the right. Here you'll find additional maps and information. The hotel and restaurant are farther down the road. I think you'll find the riding is excellent either north or south of the interstate. For additional information, call 1-800-372-3928.

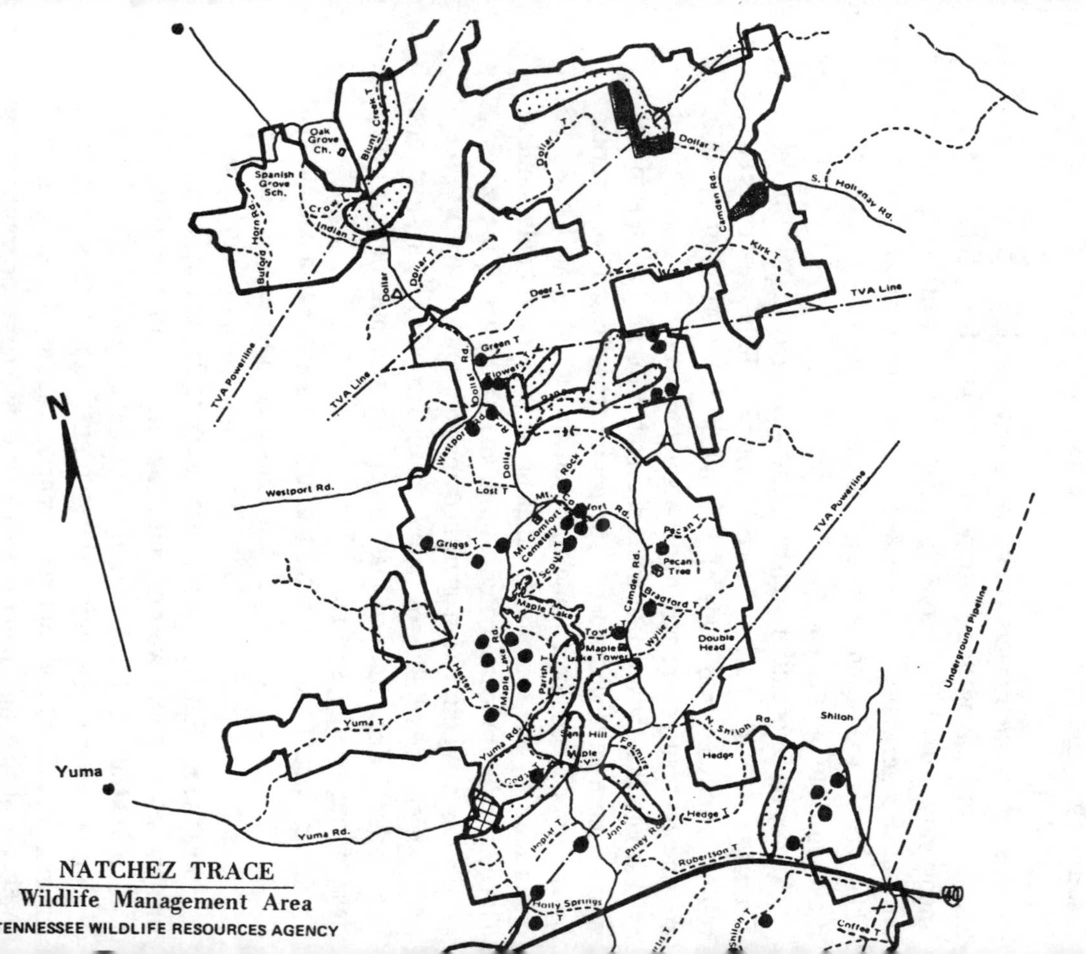
Oak Grove Ch.
Blunt Creek T
Spanish Grove Sch.
Crow
Indian T
Buford
Horn Rd.
Dollar T
Dollar
Camden Rd.
S. Holladay Rd.
Kirk T
TVA Line
Deer T
TVA Powerline
Green T
Flowers
Dollar Rd.
Westport Rd.
Rock T
Lost T
Mt. Comfort Rd.
Mt. Comfort Cemetery
Scout T
Griggs T
Pecan T
Pecan Tree
Bradford T
Wylie T
Double Head
Maple Lake
Tower T
Maple Lake Tower
Maple Lake Rd.
Parish T
Hester T
Yuma T
Yuma Rd.
Sand Hill
Fesmire T
Underground Pipeline
N. Shiloh Rd.
Shiloh
Hedge
Hedge T
Poplar T
Jones T
Piney Rd.
Robertson T
Holly Springs T
Shiloh T
Coffee T
Yuma
N
NATCHEZ TRACE
Wildlife Management Area
TENNESSEE WILDLIFE RESOURCES AGENCY

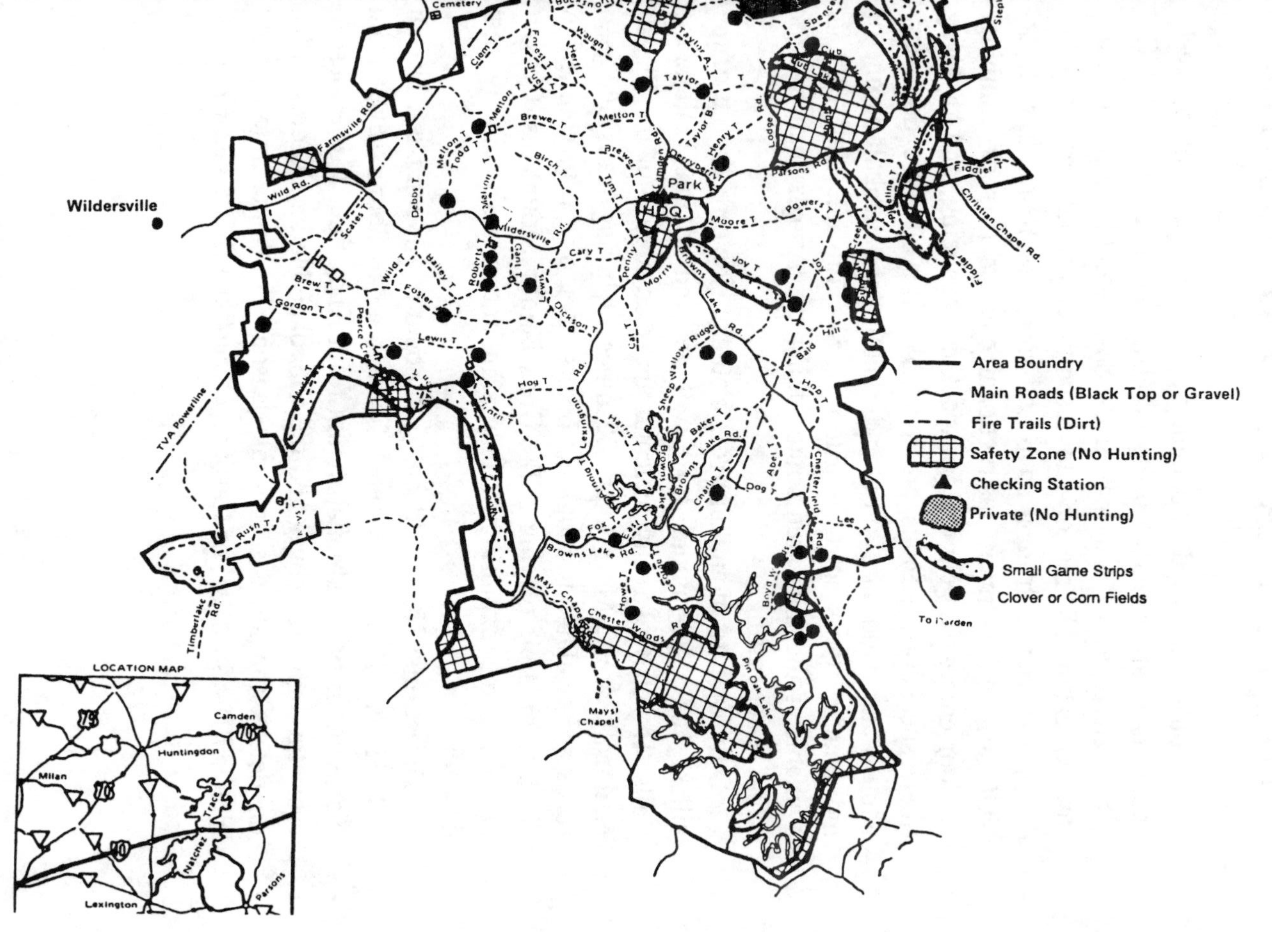

Area Boundry
Main Roads (Black Top or Gravel)
Fire Trails (Dirt)
Safety Zone (No Hunting)
Checking Station
Private (No Hunting)
Small Game Strips
Clover or Corn Fields
Wildersville
TVA Powerline
Timberlake Rd.
Farmsville Rd.
Wild Rd.
Park
HDQ.
Wildersville Rd.
Browns Lake Rd.
Sheep Wallow Ridge
Christian Chapel Rd.
Parsons Rd.
Chester Woods
Pin Oak Lake
Mays Chapel
LOCATION MAP
Camden
Huntingdon
Milan
Natchez Trace
Lexington
Parsons

NANTAHALA OUTDOOR CENTER

If you're interested in planning a great escape week or weekend, this is an excellent place to visit any time of year. NOC offers all types of lodging, from $8-per-night dorms to fully stocked cabins. Three on-site restaurants provide any type of dining experience from a soup and sandwich to rainbow trout. NOC also offers many instructional courses in rock climbing, outdoor emergency clinics, backpacking, canoeing, and kayaking (their specialty). Rentals are available. If you have done any white water paddling, you already know the Nantahala is one of the hottest rivers in the eastern U.S. Full-time day care is available if the kids aren't into hiking the Appalachian trail or white water rafting.

Only want to mountain bike? You can ride directly out of the village, or a 20-minute drive will get you to the Tsali horse trails. If you feel really adventurous, plan a ride in the Pisgah National Forest. More than 100 miles of hiking trails and jeep roads are available to mountain bikers. You owe it to yourself to spend some time playing in the Great Smoky Mountains. Get out and do some exploring, climb a mountain and enjoy a real downhill.

Directions: NOC is located just south of Bryson City, NC on US Hwy. 19/74, a mere five-and-a-half-hour drive from Nashville or two-and-a-half hours from Knoxville. It is easiest to cross through Gatlinburg and the Cherokee National Forest. Plan on delays for tourists in peak season. For more information: NOC, 704-488-2175, or Carolina Cycle Tours, 704-488-6737.

TSALI HORSE TRAILS

Long regarded as the finest mountain biking in the south, the Tsali Horse Trails offer riding almost anyone can enjoy. Not only are there many trails to explore, every corner brings a new view of Fontana Lake or the Great Smoky Mountains. There are several big climbs, but for the most part this is just nice riding. You meander among mountain ridges, following banked turns along the coves of Fontana Lake.

With four different loops available (Right Loop 11.2 mi., Left Loop 11.9 mi., Mouse Branch 7.2 mi., and Thompson Loop 7.4 mi.), this is a road trip you must make. There is a rotation system between cyclists and horses, so check the board at the trailhead of the original left and right loops to see which trails are open that day. Don't be disappointed if a specific trail is not open. Each offers an excellent mountain biking experience.

Directions to Tsali: From the junction of U.S. Hwy. 19/74 and NC 28, drive north on NC 28 for 3.6 miles. A U.S. Forest Service sign on the right marks the entrance to Tsali Recreation Area. Turn right here and drive down the gravel road 1.5 miles. Drive straight ahead to the trail head for the right and left loops.

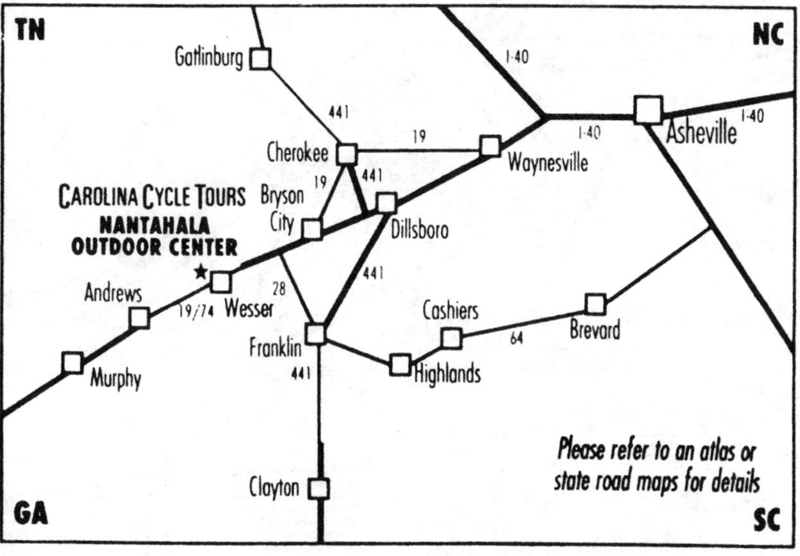

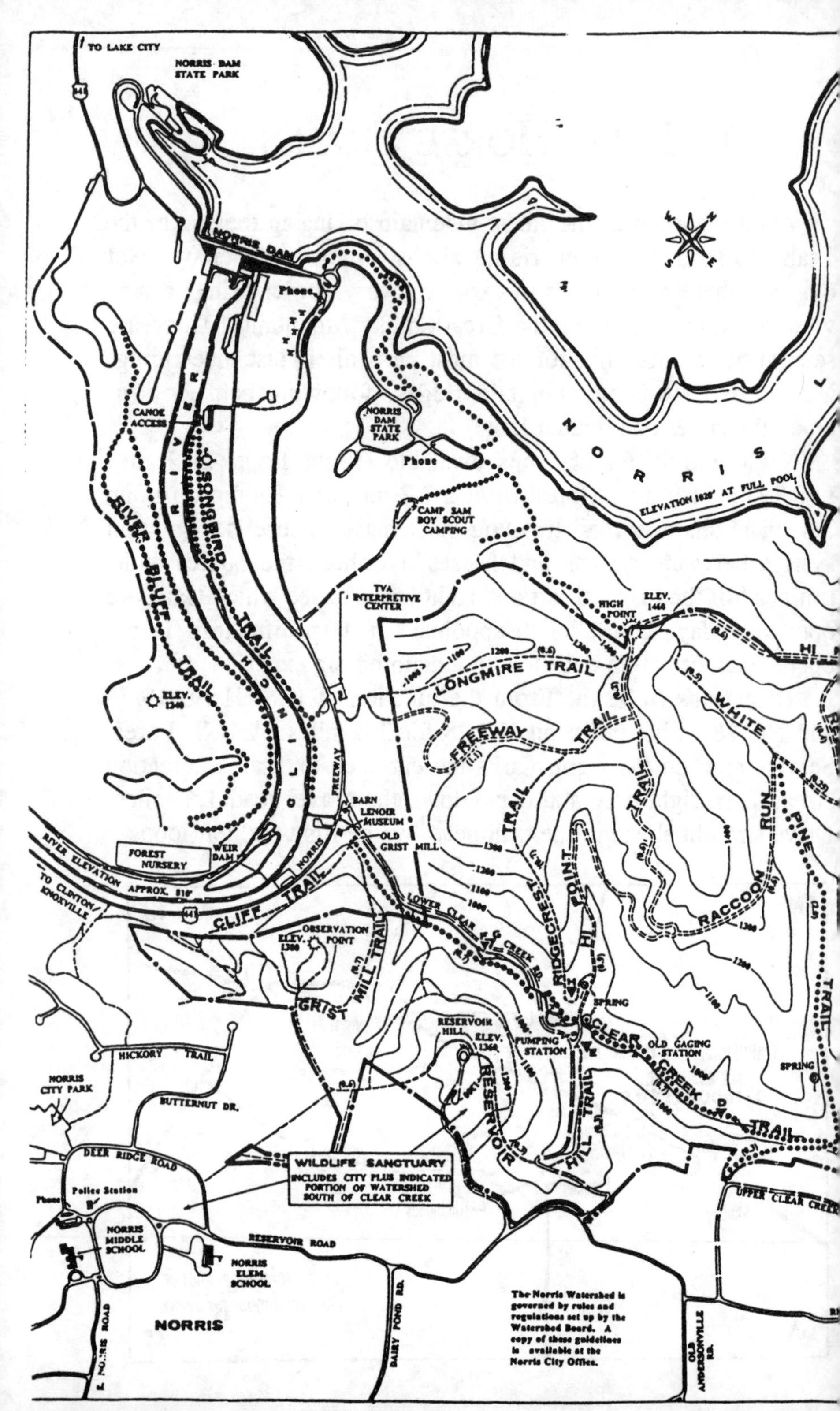

TO LAKE CITY
NORRIS DAM STATE PARK
NORRIS DAM
Phone
NORRIS DAM STATE PARK
Phone
CANOE ACCESS
RIVER
SONGBIRD TRAIL
RIVER BLUFF TRAIL
CAMP SAM BOY SCOUT CAMPING
NORRIS L
ELEVATION 1020' AT FULL POOL
TVA INTERPRETIVE CENTER
HIGH POINT
ELEV. 1460
HIGH CLIMB
ELEV. 1240
LONGMIRE TRAIL
FREEWAY TRAIL
WHITE PINE TRAIL
FREEWAY
BARN
LENOIR MUSEUM
OLD GRIST MILL
NORRIS FWY
FOREST NURSERY
WEIR DAM
RIVER ELEVATION APPROX. 810'
TO CLINTON/ KNOXVILLE
CLIFF TRAIL
RIDGECREST TRAIL
POINT HILL TRAIL
RACCOON RUN
LOWER CLEAR CREEK RD.
OBSERVATION POINT
ELEV. 1300
GRIST MILL TRAIL
SPRING
RESERVOIR HILL
ELEV. 1360
PUMPING STATION
CLEAR CREEK TRAIL
OLD GAGING STATION
SPRING
HICKORY TRAIL
NORRIS CITY PARK
BUTTERNUT DR.
RESERVOIR TRAIL
HILL TRAIL
DEER RIDGE ROAD
WILDLIFE SANCTUARY
INCLUDES CITY PLUS INDICATED PORTION OF WATERSHED SOUTH OF CLEAR CREEK
UPPER CLEAR CREEK
Police Station
Phone
NORRIS MIDDLE SCHOOL
RESERVOIR ROAD
NORRIS ELEM. SCHOOL
NORRIS
E. NORRIS ROAD
DAIRY POND RD.
OLD ANDERSONVILLE RD.
The Norris Watershed is governed by rules and regulations set up by the Watershed Board. A copy of these guidelines is available at the Norris City Office.

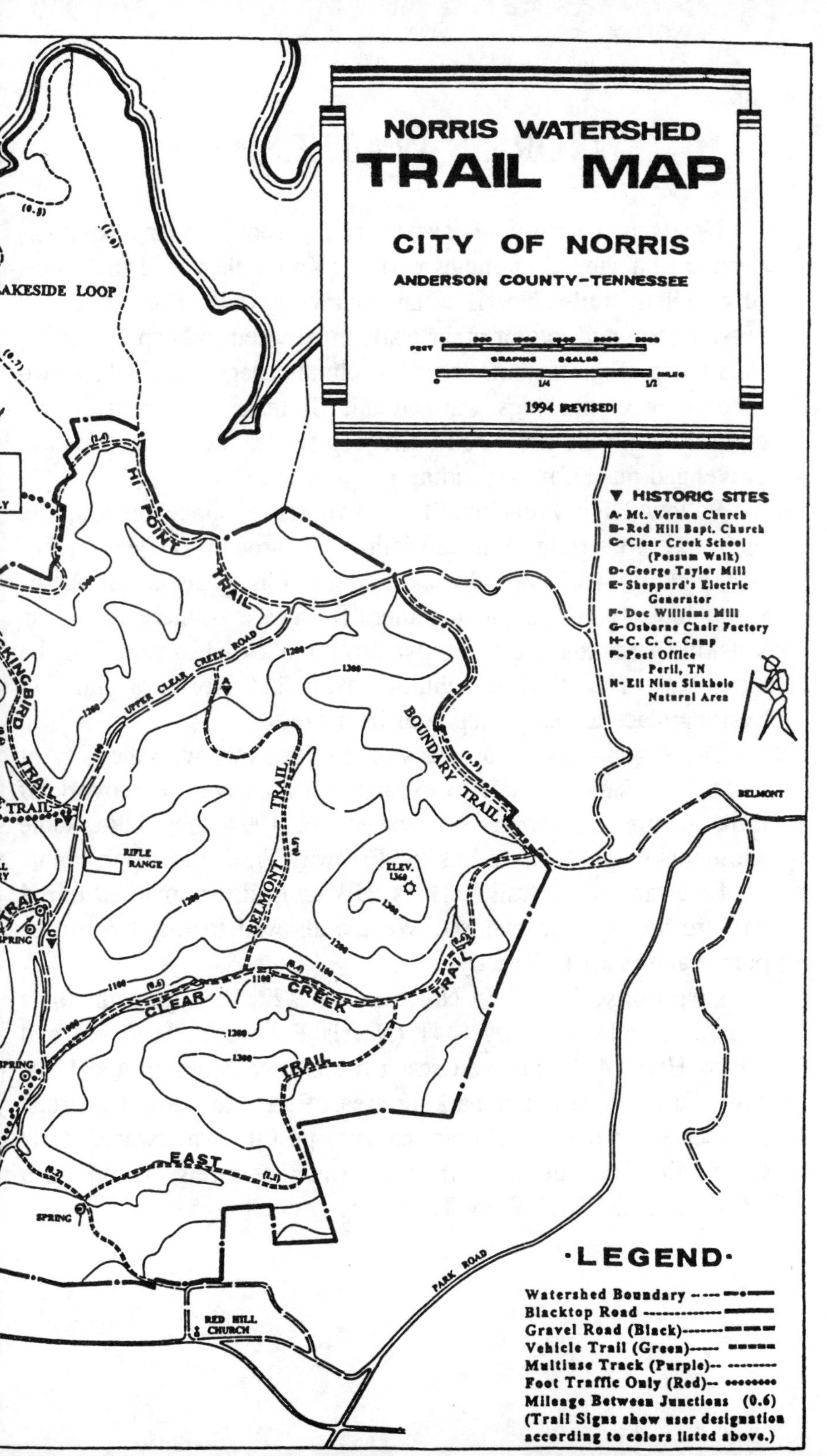

NORRIS WATERSHED
TRAIL MAP
CITY OF NORRIS
ANDERSON COUNTY-TENNESSEE
1994 (REVISED)
▼ HISTORIC SITES
A- Mt. Vernon Church
B- Red Hill Bapt. Church
C- Clear Creek School (Possum Walk)
D- George Taylor Mill
E- Sheppard's Electric Generator
F- Doe Williams Mill
G- Osborne Chair Factory
H- C. C. C. Camp
P- Post Office Peril, TN
N- Eli Nine Sinkhole Natural Area
·LEGEND·
Watershed Boundary
Blacktop Road
Gravel Road (Black)
Vehicle Trail (Green)
Multiuse Track (Purple)
Foot Traffic Only (Red)
Mileage Between Junctions (0.6)
(Trail Signs show user designation according to colors listed above.)
LAKESIDE LOOP
HI POINT TRAIL
UPPER CLEAR CREEK ROAD
BOUNDARY TRAIL
BELMONT TRAIL
CLEAR CREEK TRAIL
EAST TRAIL
RIFLE RANGE
ELEV. 1360
SPRING
BELMONT
PARK ROAD
RED HILL CHURCH

NORRIS WATERSHED

Norris is a long-time favorite riding spot of many Knoxvillians. Just a short 20 minutes north of Knoxville you'll find miles of excellent trails. Norris is laid out very well: There's a long outside loop and lots of other trails in between to keep the riding interesting. Expect some long hill climbs, beginning with a two miler to get your legs warmed up. (It makes for a great trip down.) The trails are mostly dirt jeep roads; the main roads are gravel and make for easy riding.

Follow High Point uphill for two miles. Once on top, the main trail goes right. You can follow this around to Clear Creek, then pick up Mockingbird back to High Point. This is just one of many loops you can put together. Be aware -- there are some sensitive areas marked where we are not allowed to ride. For the most part, riders of all abilities will find Norris a fun and exciting place to ride. Keep your map handy.

The Appalachian Club has worked diligently with the City of Norris and park officials to expand and improve the network of trails within the Norris Watershed. In 1994 they built some additional single track to link the Freeway Trail from High Point.

Be aware of the trail markers. Hiking trails are marked in red and are not open to cyclists. We are allowed to ride the green, purple and black trails only.

Directions: Take I-75 North to exit 122, then go right for a couple of miles to Hwy. 441 (Norris Freeway). Turn left and follow Hwy. 441 until you reach the Lenoir Museum and Grist Mill. Park in the upper parking area of the Museum. The trails are located up the gravel road that runs past the waterwheel at the Grist Mill. Ride up the hill to the water pumping station, turn left. This is the High Point Trail. Happy climbing!

OCOEE

It used to be that when someone mentioned the Ocoee River you thought of excellent white water. Today, those words conjure up images of beautiful singletrack winding its way up and down Chilhowee Mountain. A variety of trails recently have opened to mountain bikes in this area and plans for several additional trails are in the works. Currently the most popular riding is around the Chilhowee Recreations Area. The primary trails are Clear Creek, Clemmer, and Benton Falls.

Clear Creek is 5.5 miles of the best riding in the state. I suggest parking on Greasy Creek Road and starting with a 800' climb to the summit. Once there you will find a great network of hiking trails to ride. The Benton Falls trail will take you past the waterfall and get you on the other side of the Rock Creek drainage. Clemmer Trail runs along that side of the mountain and also descends to the bottom of the mountain at Greasy Creek Road.

The Oswald Dome lookout tower is a good destination if you like to climb. At 3,000' it is 1,000' above Chilhowee and 2,000' above Greasy Creek Rd. There is a good access trail off Oswald Dome Rd. near Sulphur Springs Gap. A hiking trail leads directly up a constant grade to the top. From there you can descend down Oswald Dome Rd. One branch leads back to Chilhowee Recreation Area, the other goes down to the base of the mountain for a short road ride back to your car.

If you don't want to experience all the climbing and technical sections, drive up to the recreation area and just ride the trails on top of the mountain. Don't discount the forest service roads. We have access to all gated roads in the Ocoee Ranger District.

Directions: Greasy Creek Road (Hwy. 30) is located off Hwy. 64, east of Ocoee and 3-4 miles past the Ocoee dam. To reach Chilhowee Recreation Area, take FDR 77 up Chilhowee Mtn., approx. 7 miles. Turn right at the campground and go .4 miles to the parking area. Contact the Forest Service at 423-476-9700.

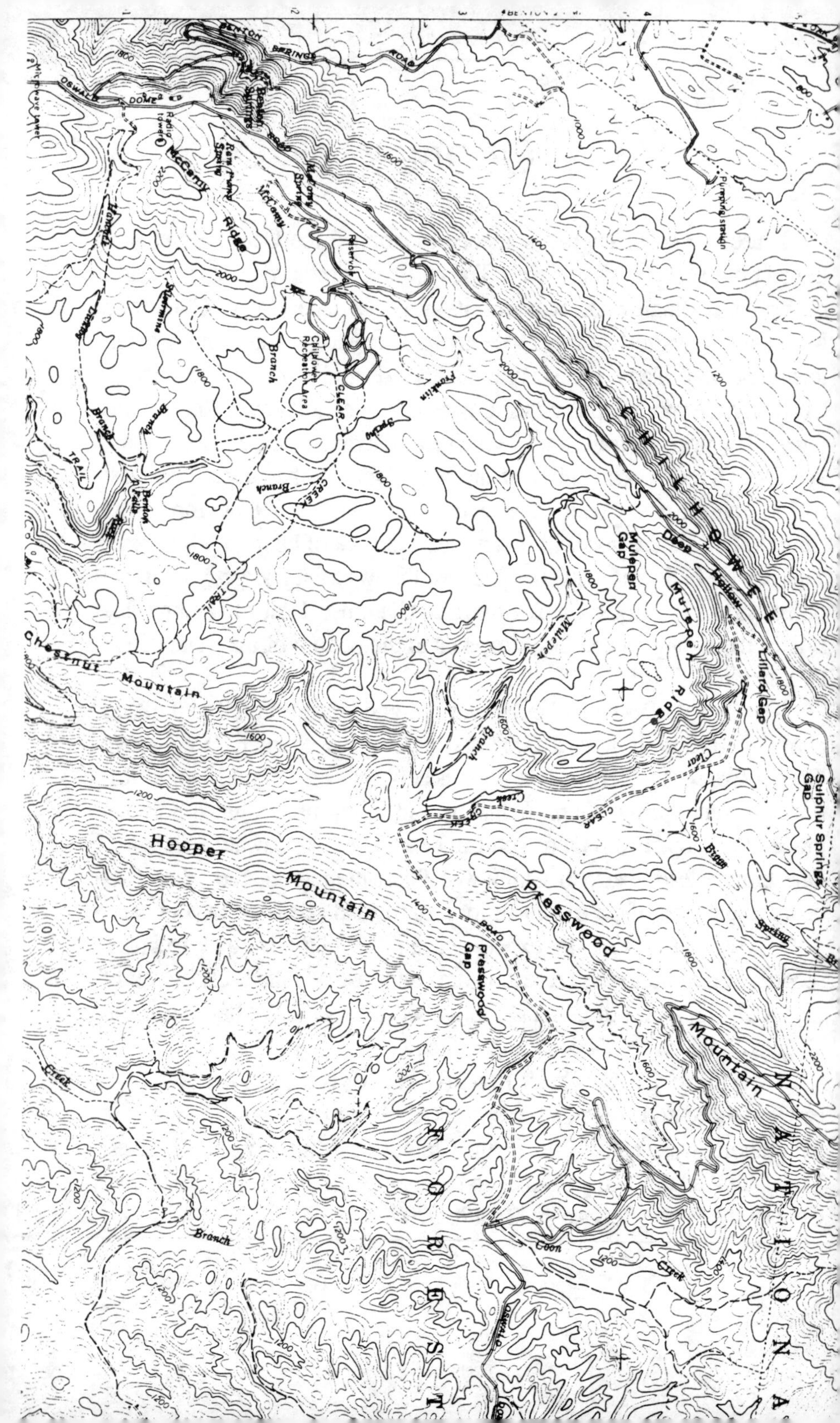

BENTON SPRINGS ROAD
OSWALD DOME RD
Radio tower
McCamy Ridge
Ram Pump Spring
McCamy Spring
McCamy
Reservoir
Chilhowee Recreation Area
CLEAR CREEK
Franklin
Spring
Branch
TRAIL
Benton Falls
Chestnut Mountain
Hooper Mountain
Presswood Gap
Presswood
Mountain
ROAD
Mulepen Gap
Mulepen Ridge
Mulepen
Deep Hollow
Lillard Gap
Sulphur Springs Gap
Clear Creek
Briggs
Spring
CHILHOWEE
Pumping station
Coon
Creek
Branch
Creek
OSWALD
F O R E S T
N A T I O N A
2000
1800
1600
1400
1200
1000
800

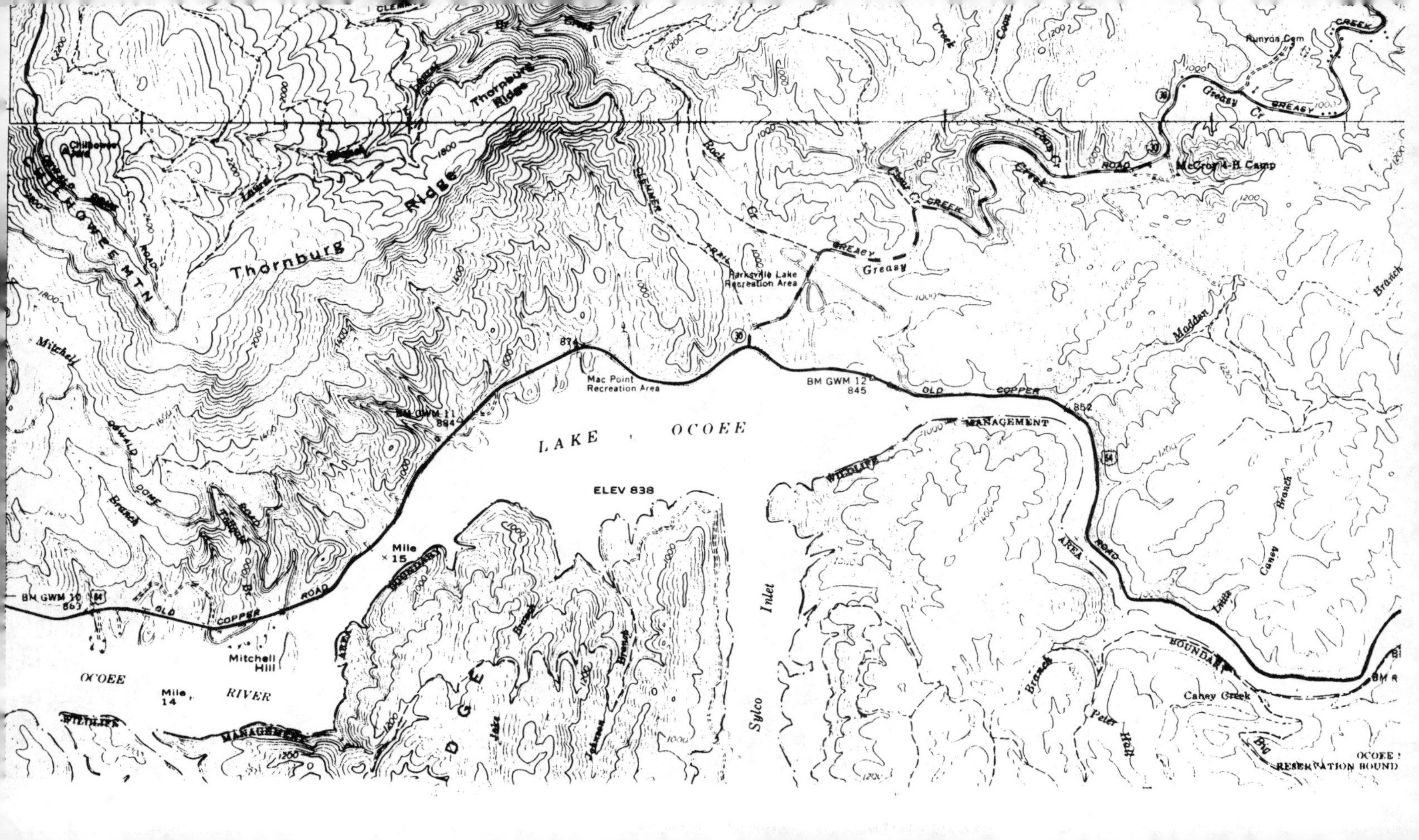

LAKE OCOEE
ELEV 838
Mac Point Recreation Area
Parksville Lake Recreation Area
BM GWM 12 845
BM GWM 11 884
BM GWM 10 863
OLD COPPER ROAD
WILDLIFE MANAGEMENT AREA ROAD
Thornburg
Thornburg Ridge
CHILHOWEE MTN
Mitchell Hill
OCOEE RIVER
Mile 14
Mile 15
Sylco Inlet
McCroy 4-H Camp
Runyon Cem
Greasy Cr
Coon Cr
Rock Cr
CLEMMER TRAIL
Caney Creek
Little Caney Branch
Peter Hall Branch
Madden Branch
Mitchell
OSWALD DOME ROAD
BOUNDARY
OCOEE RESERVATION BOUND

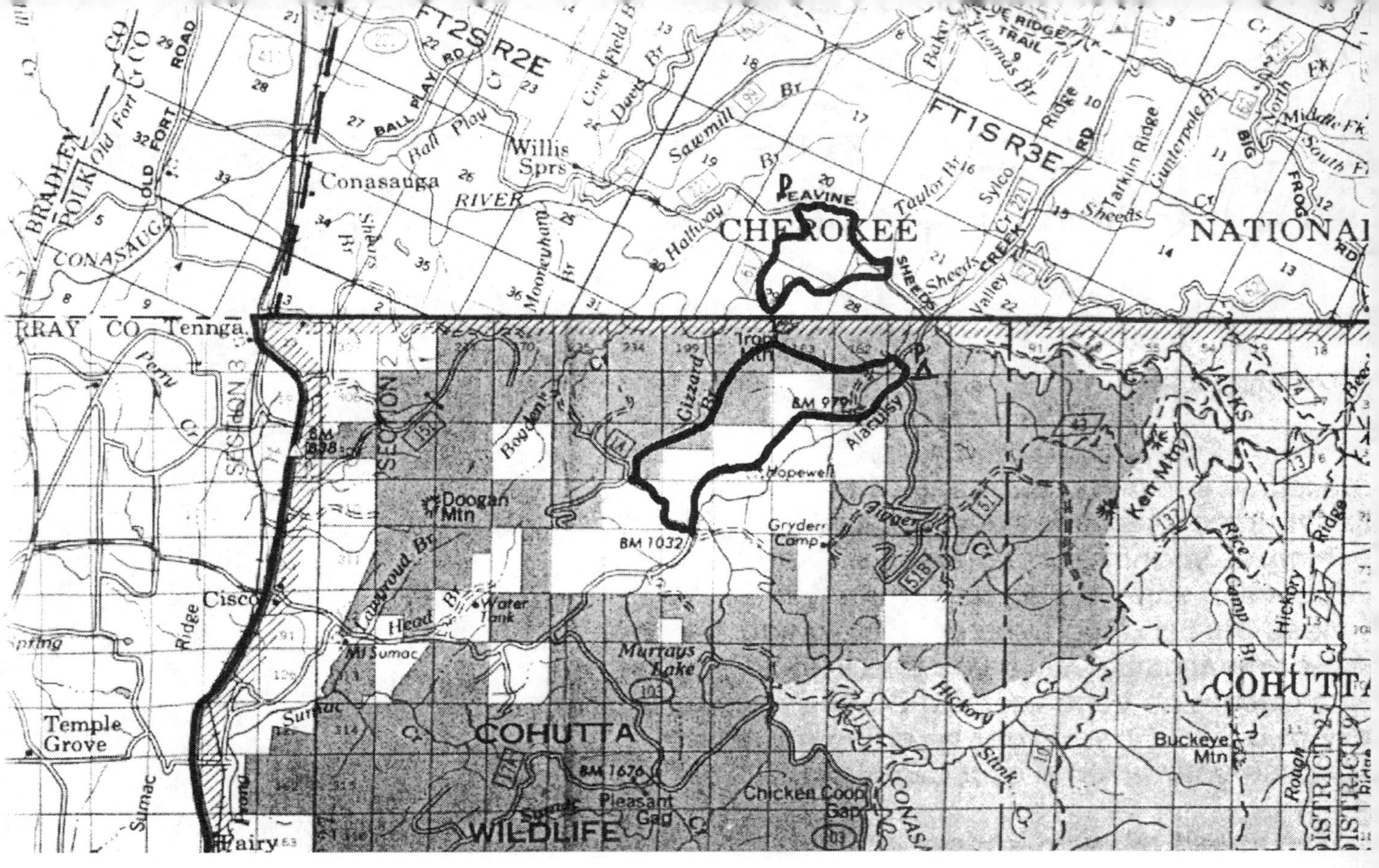
BRADLEY
POLK
CO
CONASAUGA
OLD FORT ROAD
Old Fort Cr
FT2S R2E
BALL PLAY RD
Ball Play Cr
Willis Sprs
Conasauga
RIVER
Cove Field Br
Davis Br
Sawmill Br
Halfway Br
Mooneyham Br
PEAVINE
CHEROKEE
FT1S R3E
Taylor Br
Sylco
Sheeds Cr
SHEEDS CREEK
Valley
Ridge
RD
Tarkiln Ridge
Gunterpole Br
BIG FROG
North Fk
Middle Fk
South Fk
BLUE RIDGE TRAIL
Thomas Br
Baker Cr
NATIONAL
MURRAY CO
Tennga
Perry Cr
SECTION 3
SECTION 2
BM 898
Bogden Br
Gizzard Br
Iron Mtn
BM 979
Alaculsy
Hopewell
Doogan Mtn
BM 1032
Gryder Camp
Jigger Cr
Lawroud Br
Head Br
Water Tank
Cisco
Ridge
Spring
Mt Sumac
Murrays Lake
Temple Grove
Sumac Cr
COHUTTA
BM 1676
Pleasant Gap
Chicken Coop Gap
WILDLIFE
Fairy
Sumac
Hickory Cr
Slink Cr
CONASAUGA
Ken Mtn
JACKS
Rice Camp Br
Hickory Ridge
COHUTTA
Buckeye Mtn
Rough Ridge
DISTRICT 27
DISTRICT 9

CONASAUGA RIVER TRAIL / IRON MTN. TRAIL
OCOEE NATIONAL FOREST

This is another new area recently open to mountain bikes. By combining the Conasauga trail in TN, and the Iron Mountain trail in GA, you now have a fairly easy ten mile trail one way. A twenty mile trip in the middle of the Smokies.

The Conasauga River Trail runs along the river banks for more than five miles. Originally a horse trail, it is now designated multi-use.

To access the Iron Mountain Trail, you will have to cross the river. This should not be a problem during the summer months. Many enjoy the opportunity for a swim. Now that you are in Georgia, there will be a few more hills to climb. With four more miles of singletrack and closed woods roads, you will eventually end up at the Cottonwood Patch camping area. This is a primitive camping area that has outhouses but no drinking water. You will have a few more river crossings and the terrain is rolling. However the climbs are rewarded with spectacular views of the surrounding Cohutta Mountains.

Directions: From the Ocoee Ranger Station turn right onto Hwy. 64; travel approx. 4.8 miles to County Rd. 2330 (Cookson Creek Rd.) at Cherokee Corner. Turn left and travel 3.5 miles to FDR 33711. Trailhead is on the left where parking is available. From Chatsworth, take U.S,. 411 north about 13 miles to Cisco, GA. Turn right (Greg's Store on left) and travel about 8 miles to the Iron Mountain Trailhead.

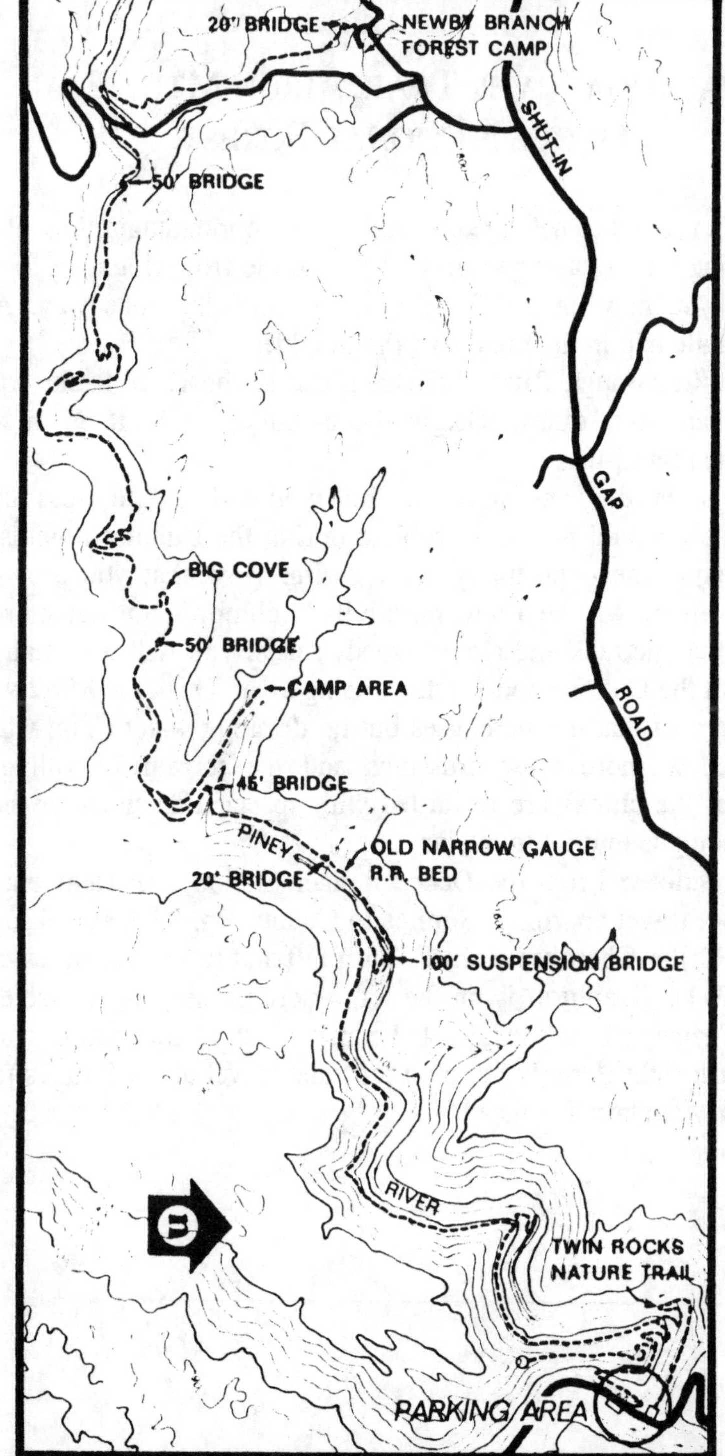
20" BRIDGE
NEWBY BRANCH
FOREST CAMP
SHUT-IN
50' BRIDGE
BIG COVE
50' BRIDGE
CAMP AREA
GAP
ROAD
45' BRIDGE
PINEY
OLD NARROW GAUGE
R.R. BED
20' BRIDGE
100' SUSPENSION BRIDGE
RIVER
TWIN ROCKS
NATURE TRAIL
PARKING AREA

PINEY RIVER TRAIL

This is a tract of land the Bowater Paper Company set aside as a recreation area. Bowater owns more than 300,000 acres of land in Tennessee. In many cases, we are allowed access for riding. Piney River caught my eye as a prime spot to visit. The main trail is 10 miles long, offering scenic trails, breathtaking overlooks, suspension bridges to cross, and several waterfalls. This is one of the most technical trails I have ridden. It is primarily a back country hiking trail and is unimproved; many areas required walking your bike. This is not a trail for beginning *or* intermediate riders.

I found this to be a beautiful and undiscovered area. While there were no super tough climbs, the loose rocks and terrain made riding very difficult in many areas. Once you commit yourself to the trail, it is very remote and would be difficult to get out of in the event of an emergency.

Just one mile from Spring City, the Twin Rocks Nature Trail is a two-and-a-half miler which overlooks the Tennessee Valley and Piney River Gorge. From here you can pick up the Piney River Trail and ride to Newby Branch Forest Camp. If you've had enough, take the road home, or turn around to complete a 20-mile ride. You could also have a pickup car at the camping area.

Directions: Going east from downtown Spring City on Hwy. 68, go one mile east and turn left on Shut-in Gap Road. The Twin Rocks parking area is on the left one mile from the turn. The turn-off for Newby Branch Camp is 5.3 miles farther. Go left and follow this 0.7 miles, and take the third left turn into the camping area.

Please stay on designated trails to avoid trampling native vegetation. Minimize potential erosion to trails by not using muddy trails or short-cutting switch backs.

PIGEON MOUNTAIN

Located just south of the Tennessee state line, Pigeon Mountain is a mountain biker's mecca that has only been ridden by a few locals until now. Pigeon Mountain is a Georgia W.M.A. that is only open to horses, hikers and mountain bikers. The trails are mostly single track horse trails; some are jeep and logging roads. For the most part, the trails are rough, rocky, steep, and demanding.

There is a variety of well-marked trails running up, down and along Pigeon Mountain. The Yellow trail runs nearly 15 miles along the bluffs overlooking Lookout Mountain to the west. From High Point, you are 1,200 feet above the valley floor below, looking over the grueling climb you have just finished.

The Orange, Pink and Green trails traverse up and down the mountain. If you are not prepared for an hour-and-a-half climb, don't head down these trails. If you are looking for an extremely exciting and tough day, go for it. We began climbing up the Green trail leading past Branch Falls. The Pink trail runs over the top of the falls and heads up the mountain. Don't take this trail. It is not rideable. After climbing through "The Pocket," we picked up the Blue trail and finally reached the summit after a very long climb. The conditions ranged from Hike-A-Biking to sitting in the saddle pushing mile after mile on rugged single-track trails. On top is McCutchin Springs road and intersection of the Yellow, Orange, and Blue trails.

Now you can follow the Yellow trail even higher. After even more climbing you are rewarded when reaching High Point. This is a great place for lunch with scenic views of the valley below and Lookout Mountain directly across the valley. This is mostly rocky single track that is steady climbing until you reach High Point. The views are inspiring. If you have the legs I highly recommend this trail. We also made a side trip to Rocktown. If you have time, hike down here for some cool rock formations. (No bikes allowed)

To get back to the parking area at Estelle, return to the main junction on McCutchens Spring Road and the Blue and Yellow trails. Follow the road for about 75 yards and look for Cane Trail (orange) on the left. Be warned: This is rough, tough rocky riding, but it's mostly downhill. When you reach the junction at Bluebird Gap (blue), turn right up the hill. Your next junction will be a gravel road leading to the right; turn here and it is downhill to the parking area at Estelle. This is a 20-25 mile ride that will take most experienced riders at least five hours. There is no water available so bring your own. Again, this is extremely remote riding. Be prepared with tools and plenty of food and water.

Directions: From Nashville, I-24 south to I-59 south. Exit at Trenton and turn left. Follow Hwy. 136 through town and continue on past Cloudland Canyon SP. Turn right on Hwy. 193 and continue past Hog Jowl Rd. The Estelle camping and parking area will be on your right. From Chattanooga come through Lafayette, GA, on Hwy. 193 for four miles. When your reach Chamberlain Rd. turn right for two miles and look for the Estelle Camping area on your left. You can also park on top of the mountain to avoid having to make the big climbs. For more information, call 706-295-6041.

TICK CHECK

Lyme disease is not a common problem, but we are susceptible because of the contact we have with ticks. The best offense is a good defense. Spray yourself with a repellent containing DEET. Wear light colored clothing and look for ticks each time you stop.

Telltale symptoms of individuals infected with lyme disease is a circular "bulls-eye" rash noticeable one to 30 days after being bitten. The treatment is simple if caught early, so be aware of the problem and wear your bug spray. DEET should be used sparingly on children and not at all on infants younger than 1 year old.

CROCKFORD
PIGEON MOUNTAIN
WILDLIFE MANAGEMENT AREA

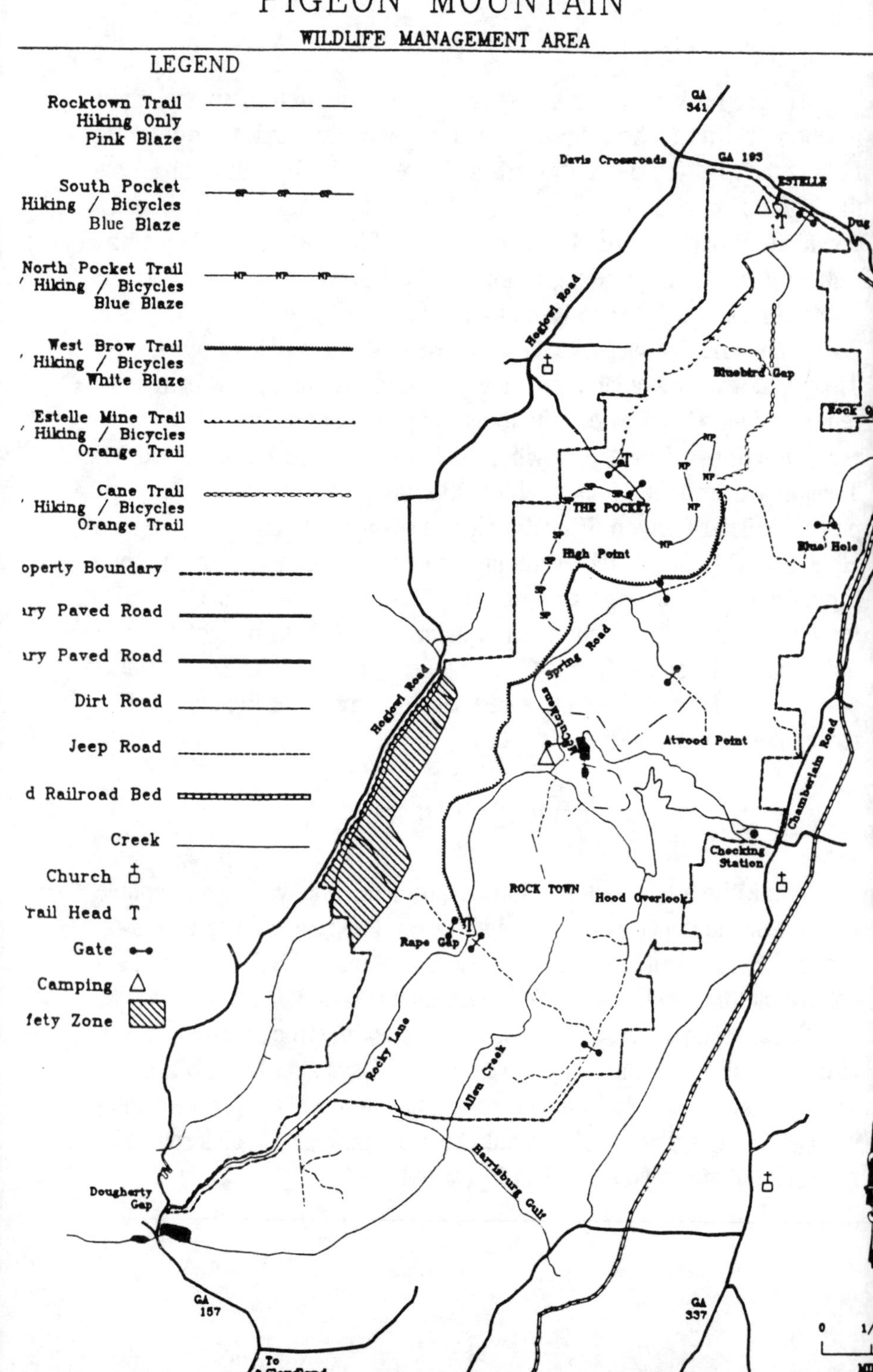

PISGAH NATIONAL FOREST

Located in the heart of the Smoky Mountains, Pisgah offers 157,000 acres and nearly 400 miles of hiking trails for recreational users. Mountain bikers are welcome here and have access to nearly half of the hiking trails throughout the National Forest. We are a new user group, and the park's current policy is that we may ride on any open or closed roads and trails not specifically closed to us. (Lists are available.)

With elevation changes from 2,000' to 6,410' at Richland Balsam Mountain and 48 different hiking trails currently available to ride, there is something here for everyone. A few of the more popular trails include Upper and Lower Sidehill and the Bent Creek area where you will find a variety of terrain and trails. For a more advanced ride, head to the North Mills River Area. Make the super tough climb up Trace Ridge to Spencer Branch Trail. Follow it until you reach the Fletcher Fields trail which will lead you back to your car after an extreme 18-20 miler.

For more information contact: Pisgah Ranger District, 704-877-3265. Maps and trail and camping information are readily available.

Also contact Carolina Cycle Tours, 41 Hwy. 19 West, Bryson City, NC 28713, at 704-488-6737.

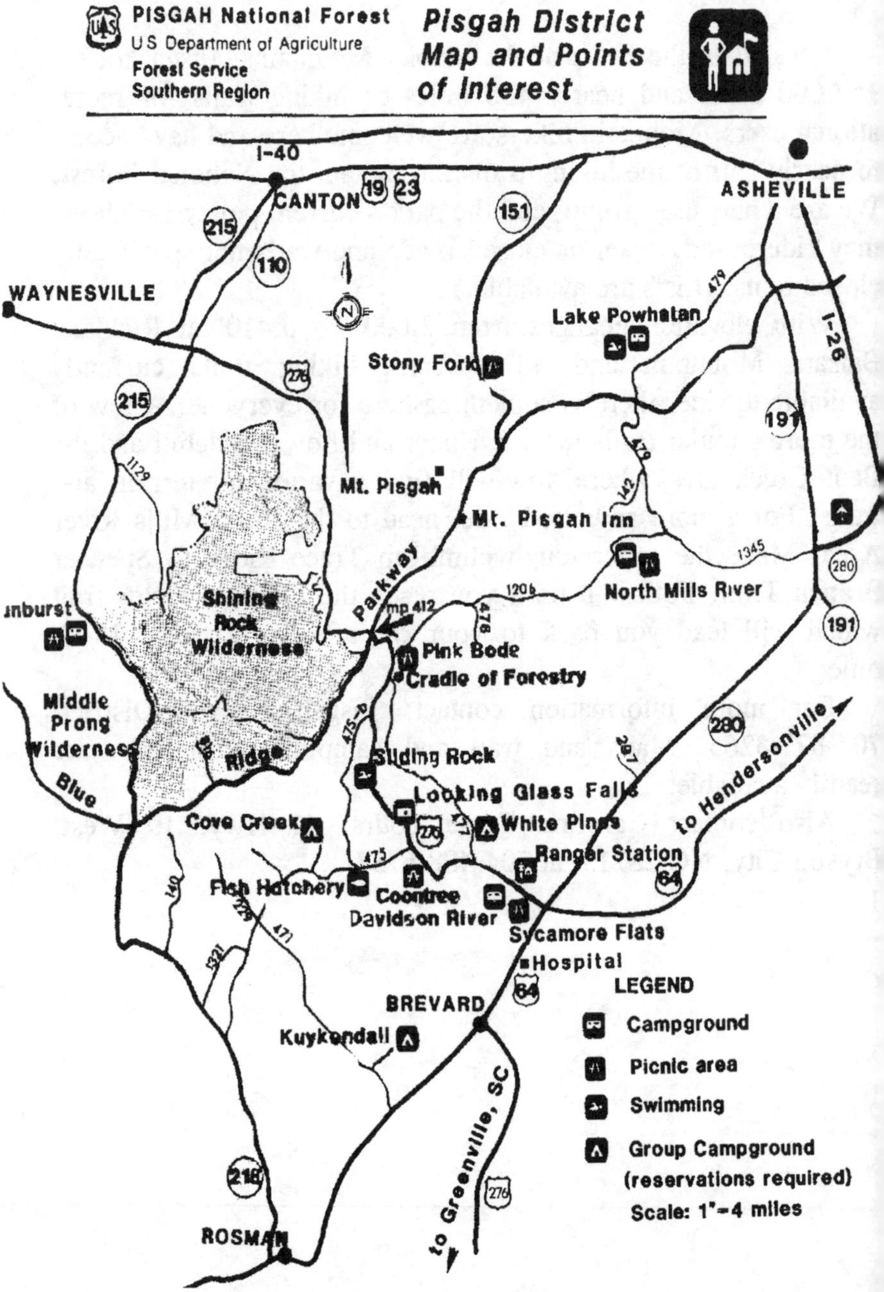

PISGAH National Forest
U S Department of Agriculture
Forest Service
Southern Region

Pisgah District Map and Points of Interest

I-40
CANTON
19
23
ASHEVILLE
215
151
110
WAYNESVILLE
Lake Powhatan
479
I-26
Stony Fork
276
215
191
1129
479
Mt. Pisgah
142
Mt. Pisgah Inn
Parkway
1345
North Mills River
280
1206
Shining Rock Wilderness
mp 412
478
191
unburst
Pink Bode
Cradle of Forestry
Middle Prong Wilderness
475-b
280
Ridge
297
Sliding Rock
Blue
to Hendersonville
Looking Glass Falls
Cove Creek
276
White Pines
Ranger Station
475
Fish Hatchery
Coontree
64
140
Davidson River
471
Sycamore Flats
1321
Hospital
64
BREVARD
Kuykendall
to Greenville, SC
215
276
ROSMAN

LEGEND

- Campground
- Picnic area
- Swimming
- Group Campground (reservations required)

Scale: 1"=4 miles

PRENTICE COOPER S.F.

Prentice Cooper State Forest, consisting of 24,000 acres just 10 miles northwest of Chattanooga, stretches north along Walden Ridge along the Cumberland Plateau. Chattanooga riders are blessed with another local area offering endless miles of jeep roads and trails. Divided by Tower Road, a 12-mile rolling gravel road, you can to access many possible loops all along it. The east side has many access roads leading to overlooks and rides along the bluffs. Lusk Point is a good destination overlooking Chattanooga. You can make a nice loop riding along Brow Road along the top of the gorge and ride Sulphur or Braddison back to Tower Road. Further south, Pot Point is another beautiful overlook that is easily accessible.

The west side is accessed by surviving the steep and technical 700-foot descent, then ascent back up the other side on Haley Road. You have to want to reach the other side. Mullins Creek is a wet crossing at the bottom; it could be dangerous during high water. The two main left turns will lead you to Elder Point, then Long Point overlooks. The left just before the descent on Haley Road will take you to another plateau with a loop trail and additional networks of smaller trails. North of Haley is yet another network of trails. Persimmon Road is the primary road on the north side. It connects to Tower Road just south of Hwy. 27.

This is a Wildlife Management Area, giving hunters first rights. Plan to stay away during Big Game season. They also close several mountains each spring for turkey nesting. Check the office for specific dates.

Directions: From Chattanooga, take Hwy. 27 north toward Whitwell. The main entrance to the park will be on your left. The Headquarters is located several miles down the main road. Stop in and ask the rangers about trails that suit your riding abilities. You can also reach the south side of the park from Hwy. 41.
USGS Quads-Wauhatchie and Ketner Gap.

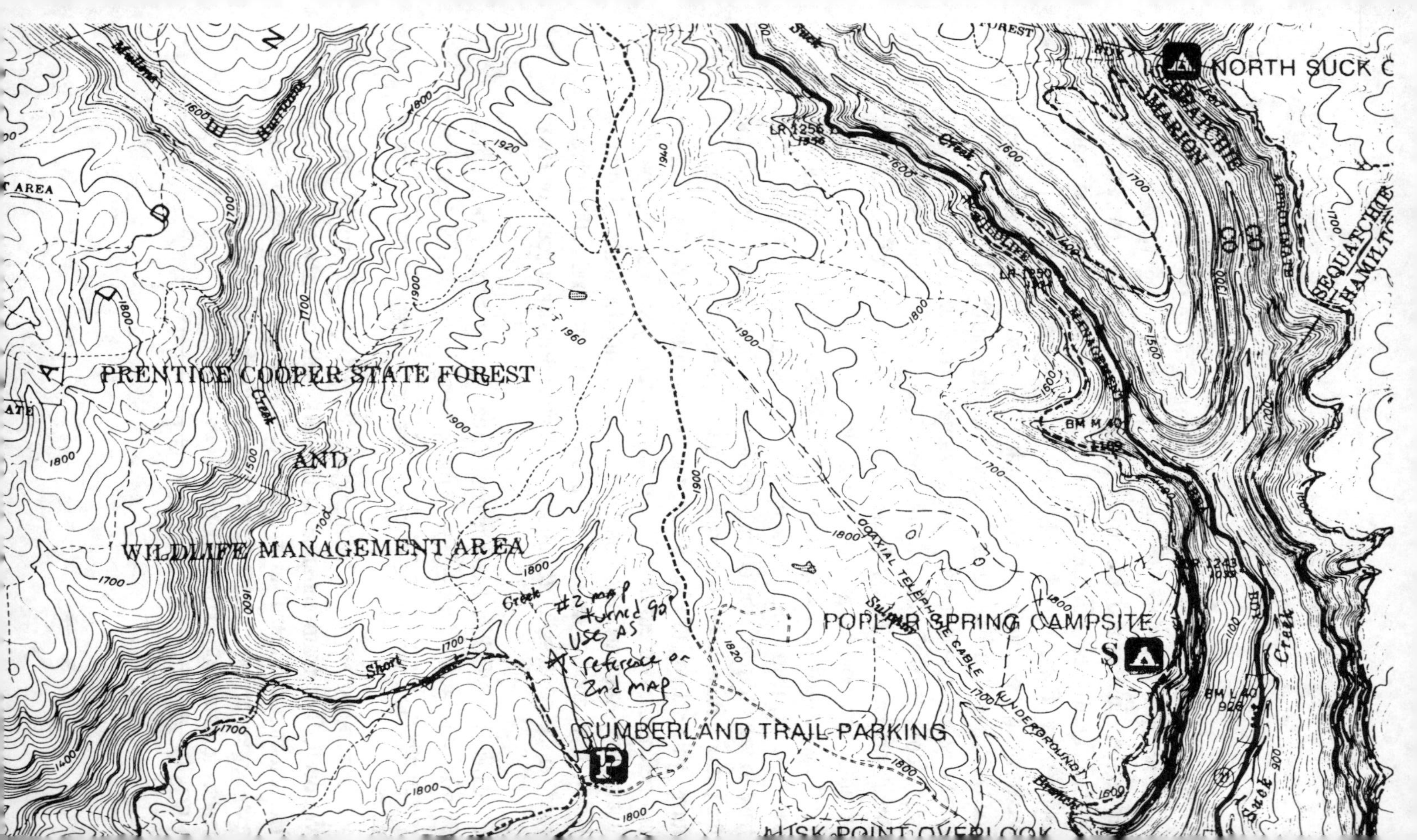

NORTH SUCK C
SEQUATCHIE
MARION
CO
CO
SEQUATCHIE
HAMILTO
APPROXIMATE
WILDLIFE MANAGEMENT
Suck Creek
Mullens
Harrison
Creek
Creek
Short
Sulphur
Branch
LR 1256
LR 1250
BM M 40
BM L 40
PRENTICE COOPER STATE FOREST
AND
WILDLIFE MANAGEMENT AREA
COAXIAL TELEPHONE CABLE
UNDERGROUND
POPLAR SPRING CAMPSITE
CUMBERLAND TRAIL PARKING
#2 map turned 90° Use as reference or 2nd map

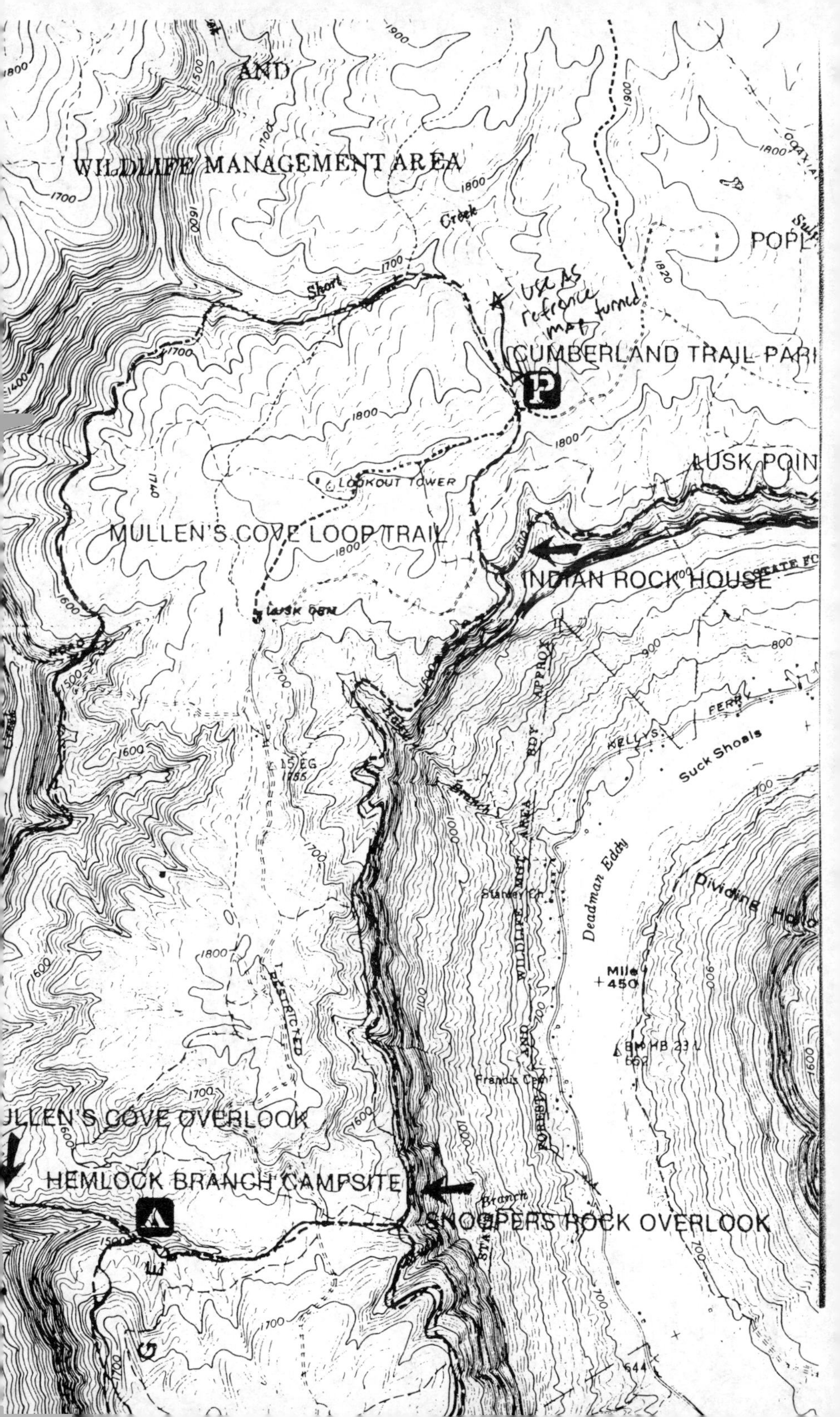

AND
WILDLIFE MANAGEMENT AREA
Short
Creek
POPL
Use as reference map turned
CUMBERLAND TRAIL PARK
LOOKOUT TOWER
LUSK POINT
MULLEN'S COVE LOOP TRAIL
INDIAN ROCK HOUSE
STATE FOREST
ROAD
KELLYS FERRY
Suck Shoals
Deadman Eddy
Dividing Hollow
Mile 450
BM HB 23 L 662
Francis Cem
Stanley Cem
WILDLIFE MGT AREA
RESTRICTED
ULLEN'S COVE OVERLOOK
HEMLOCK BRANCH CAMPSITE
SNOOPERS ROCK OVERLOOK
Branch

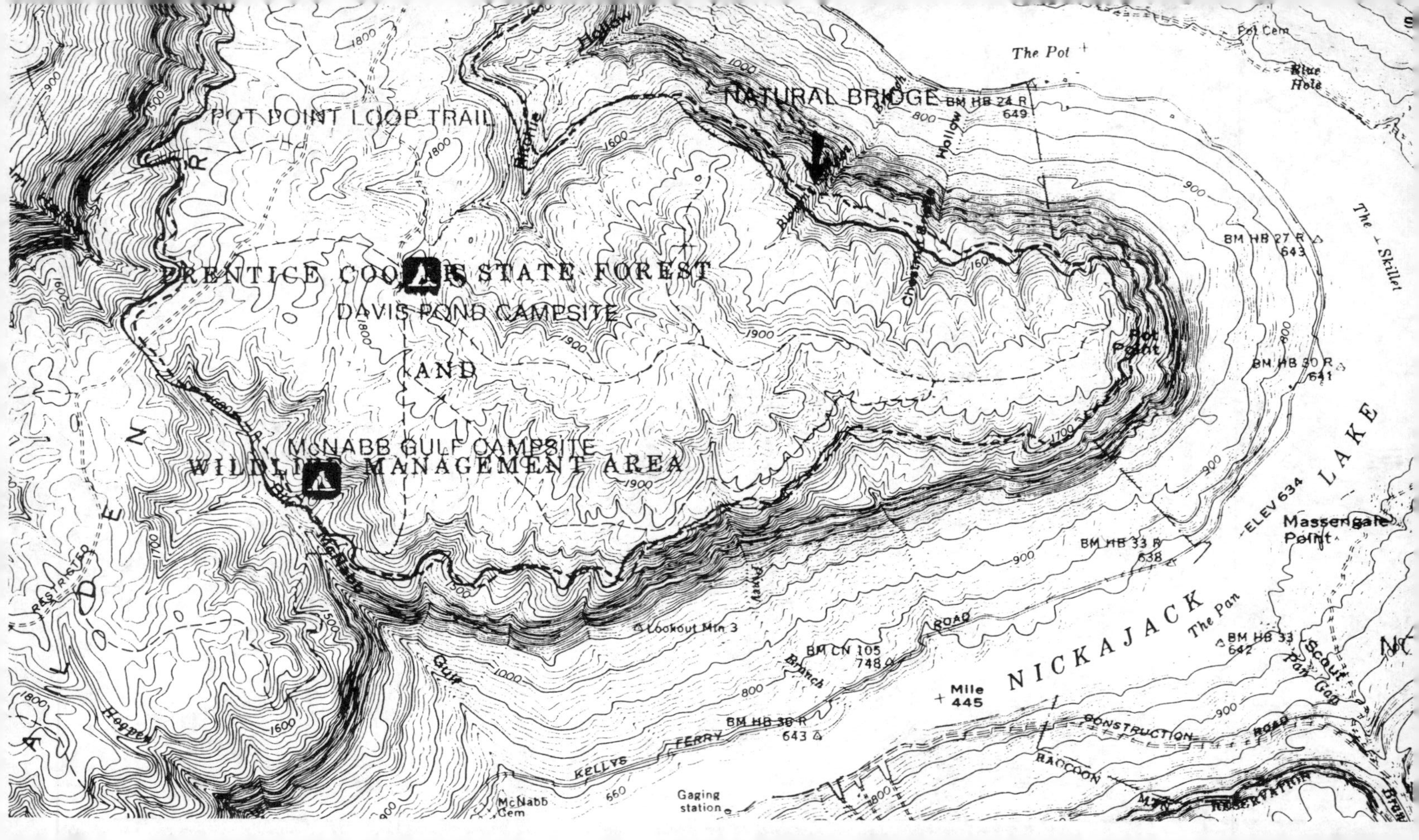

POT POINT LOOP TRAIL
NATURAL BRIDGE
PRENTICE COOPER STATE FOREST
DAVIS POND CAMPSITE
AND
McNABB GULF CAMPSITE
WILDLIFE MANAGEMENT AREA
The Pot
Pot Cem
Blue Hole
The Skillet
BM HB 24 R
649
BM HB 27 R
643
BM HB 30 R
641
Pot Point
Chestnut Branch
Hollow
Ritchie
Hollow
Massengale Point
ELEV 634
LAKE
NICKAJACK
The Pan
BM HB 33 R
638
BM HB 33
642
Scout
Pan Gap
Mile
445
Lookout Mtn 3
BM CN 105
748
Branch
Piney
BM HB 30 R
643
KELLYS FERRY ROAD
CONSTRUCTION ROAD
RACCOON
RESERVATION
Gaging station
McNabb Cem
McNabb
Gulf
Hoppen
RESTRICTED

ROTARY PARK

This is the Clarksville rider's best-kept secret. I couldn't believe this park is located in the city limits. Although K-Mart and Wendy's are within walking distance, once inside the gates you'll think you're miles from any city. Rotary isn't the largest area to ride in Tennessee, but you'll find more trails per acre than anywhere else I've ridden.

The main trail runs through a valley along a small creek. From there, anything goes. Everyone will find something they like from creek and log crossings, wide jeep roads, single track, and plenty of steep ups and downs. This is the kind of place a novice rider can come and gain experience and confidence riding in technical situations.

The Rotary Club owns this property which is used by all types of groups. There are picnic shelters and restrooms, places to grill out or play baseball. You'll be sharing the trails with horses and hikers so use common sense when you come upon them.

Directions: Take I-24 West to exit 11, Hwy. 76, then left for 3.5 miles. When you go past K-Mart, the entrance is just a couple hundred yards on the left. Most of the time the gate is closed, so park there. You'll see where most riders enter the park. As soon as you ride up this hill, the single track starts on your right. Follow this trail down and head toward the river once you reach the main road.

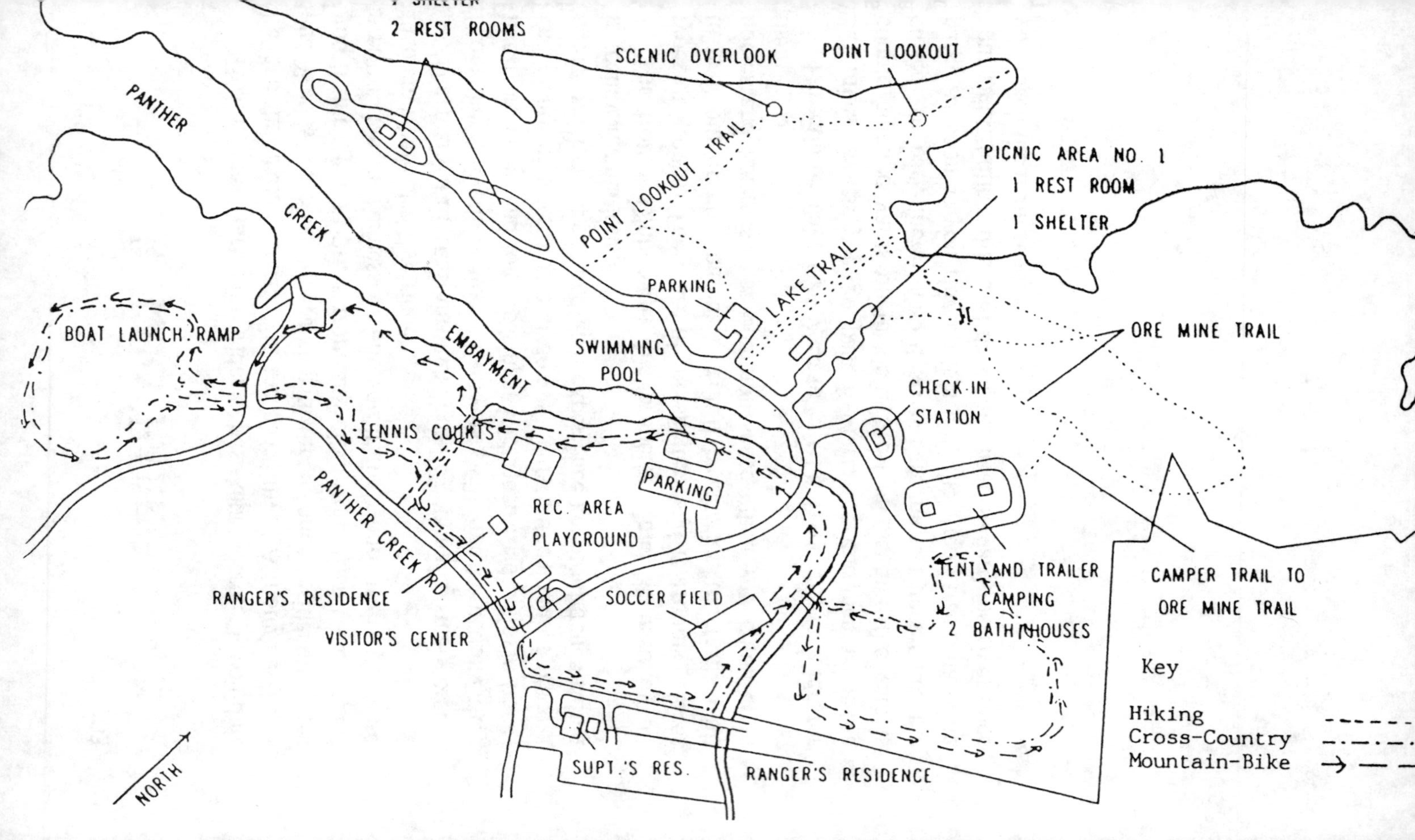
2 REST ROOMS
SCENIC OVERLOOK
POINT LOOKOUT
PANTHER
CREEK
POINT LOOKOUT TRAIL
PICNIC AREA NO. 1
1 REST ROOM
1 SHELTER
LAKE TRAIL
PARKING
BOAT LAUNCH RAMP
EMBAYMENT
SWIMMING
POOL
ORE MINE TRAIL
CHECK-IN
STATION
TENNIS COURTS
PARKING
PANTHER CREEK RD
REC. AREA
PLAYGROUND
TENT AND TRAILER
CAMPING
2 BATHHOUSES
CAMPER TRAIL TO
ORE MINE TRAIL
RANGER'S RESIDENCE
SOCCER FIELD
VISITOR'S CENTER
Key
Hiking
Cross-Country
Mountain-Bike
NORTH
SUPT.'S RES.
RANGER'S RESIDENCE

PANTHER CREEK STATE PARK

Located along the shores of Cherokee Lake is one of the newest riding areas in Tennessee. Panther Creek Recreation Area is fast becoming a popular destination for off-road recreational riders. With trails that lack the big hill climbs East Tennessee has become known for, many intermediate riders enjoy the easier pace and the chance to soak in the scenery.

Currently there are nearly six miles of trails open for mountain biking. The primary trail is the cross country course running through the park. Cyclists are not allowed to ride the Ore Mine or Point Overlook trails, although I encourage you to hike up to the overlook along the lake. I spoke with park officials who encouraged our use but cautioned against riding when trail conditions were wet or muddy. The Appalachian Club has built several additional miles of trails recently, and there are a lot of interested parties watching our activities since this is one of the few State Parks that allow mountain biking. Please keep this in mind when you don't think it matters if you ride that closed trail.

Panther Creek offers many additional activities to enjoy while you're here. After riding you can cool off in the pool or swim in the lake. Tennis, soccer, and ball fields are also available. If you want to spend the night, there are plenty of campsites and bath houses with hot showers.

Directions: Panther Creek is accessible from Interstate 81, U.S. 11E, and U.S. 25E. From I-81 take Exit 4 (White Pine Rd.) 11.5 miles to Hwy. 11E. From Highway 11E take Highway 342 W. two miles to the park entrance. The park is about six miles west of Morristown and 40 miles northeast of Knoxville.

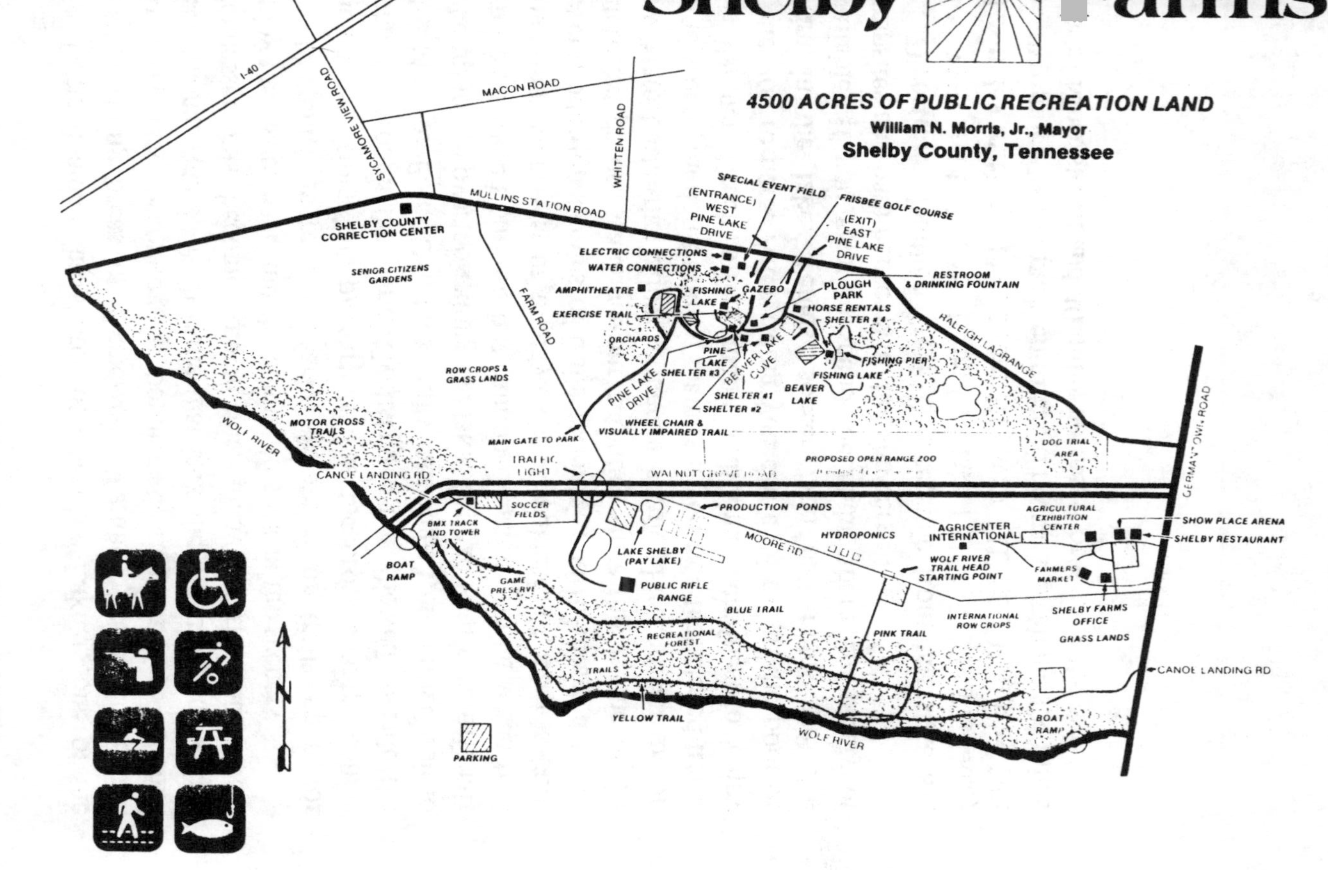
4500 ACRES OF PUBLIC RECREATION LAND
William N. Morris, Jr., Mayor
Shelby County, Tennessee
I-40
MACON ROAD
SYCAMORE VIEW ROAD
WHITTEN ROAD
MULLINS STATION ROAD
SHELBY COUNTY CORRECTION CENTER
SENIOR CITIZENS GARDENS
SPECIAL EVENT FIELD
(ENTRANCE) WEST PINE LAKE DRIVE
FRISBEE GOLF COURSE
(EXIT) EAST PINE LAKE DRIVE
ELECTRIC CONNECTIONS
WATER CONNECTIONS
AMPHITHEATRE
FISHING LAKE
GAZEBO
PLOUGH PARK
RESTROOM & DRINKING FOUNTAIN
EXERCISE TRAIL
HORSE RENTALS
SHELTER #4
ORCHARDS
PINE LAKE
SHELTER #3
BEAVER LAKE COVE
FISHING PIER
FISHING LAKE
RALEIGH LAGRANGE
FARM ROAD
ROW CROPS & GRASS LANDS
PINE LAKE DRIVE
SHELTER #1
SHELTER #2
BEAVER LAKE
WHEEL CHAIR & VISUALLY IMPAIRED TRAIL
MAIN GATE TO PARK
MOTOR CROSS TRAILS
WOLF RIVER
TRAFFIC LIGHT
DOG TRIAL AREA
PROPOSED OPEN RANGE ZOO
CANOE LANDING RD
WALNUT GROVE ROAD
GERMANTOWN ROAD
SOCCER FIELDS
PRODUCTION PONDS
BMX TRACK AND TOWER
AGRICULTURAL EXHIBITION CENTER
SHOW PLACE ARENA
AGRICENTER INTERNATIONAL
HYDROPONICS
SHELBY RESTAURANT
MOORE RD
LAKE SHELBY (PAY LAKE)
BOAT RAMP
WOLF RIVER TRAIL HEAD STARTING POINT
FARMERS MARKET
GAME PRESERVE
PUBLIC RIFLE RANGE
BLUE TRAIL
INTERNATIONAL ROW CROPS
SHELBY FARMS OFFICE
GRASS LANDS
RECREATIONAL FOREST
PINK TRAIL
TRAILS
CANOE LANDING RD
YELLOW TRAIL
BOAT RAMP
WOLF RIVER
N
PARKING

SHELBY FARMS

Shelby Farms is a gift from the citizens of Shelby County to themselves. It provides many activities for the Memphis area including soccer fields, an arboretum, an outdoor amphitheater, fishing ponds, areas to canoe, and good trails for mountain biking.

Currently 4,500 acres are available as a recreation area. The city also owns a 600 foot buffer zone of property running for several miles along the Wolf River. Hopefully this will be the next area with trails for us to use. The Memphis Office of Planning and Development is proposing 26 miles of hiking trails along the river. This will be the Wolf River Wilderness Area, consisting of 11,000 acres.

Presently, the two mountain bike trails are the Yellow and Blue trails in Shelby Farms. They are single-track hiking trails and get a lot of use. Shelby Park is home to many races throughout the year. When you're riding you'll see everyone from families out for a recreational ride to racers practicing for their next event. Keep in mind that hikers, horses, and others use the trails. **Yield the trail.**

There is supposed to be a hiking trail that runs from Shelby Farms to Kennedy Park. It's not on any maps but look for 10-12 miles along the river to ride. This is private property, so use common sense.

The Wolf River bottoms is the area the Shelby County Conservation Committee is planning to turn into a wilderness area. Supposedly there are miles of horse and four-wheeler trails to ride.

WHAT TO DO?

You just drove for over an hour to get to your favorite trail only to find out it's too wet to ride. Don't ride the muddy trails. Don't go home. Get out there and pull some trail maintenance. This is a good time to fix some of the spots water collects and lots of other problems our trails have. Trust me, it is fun.

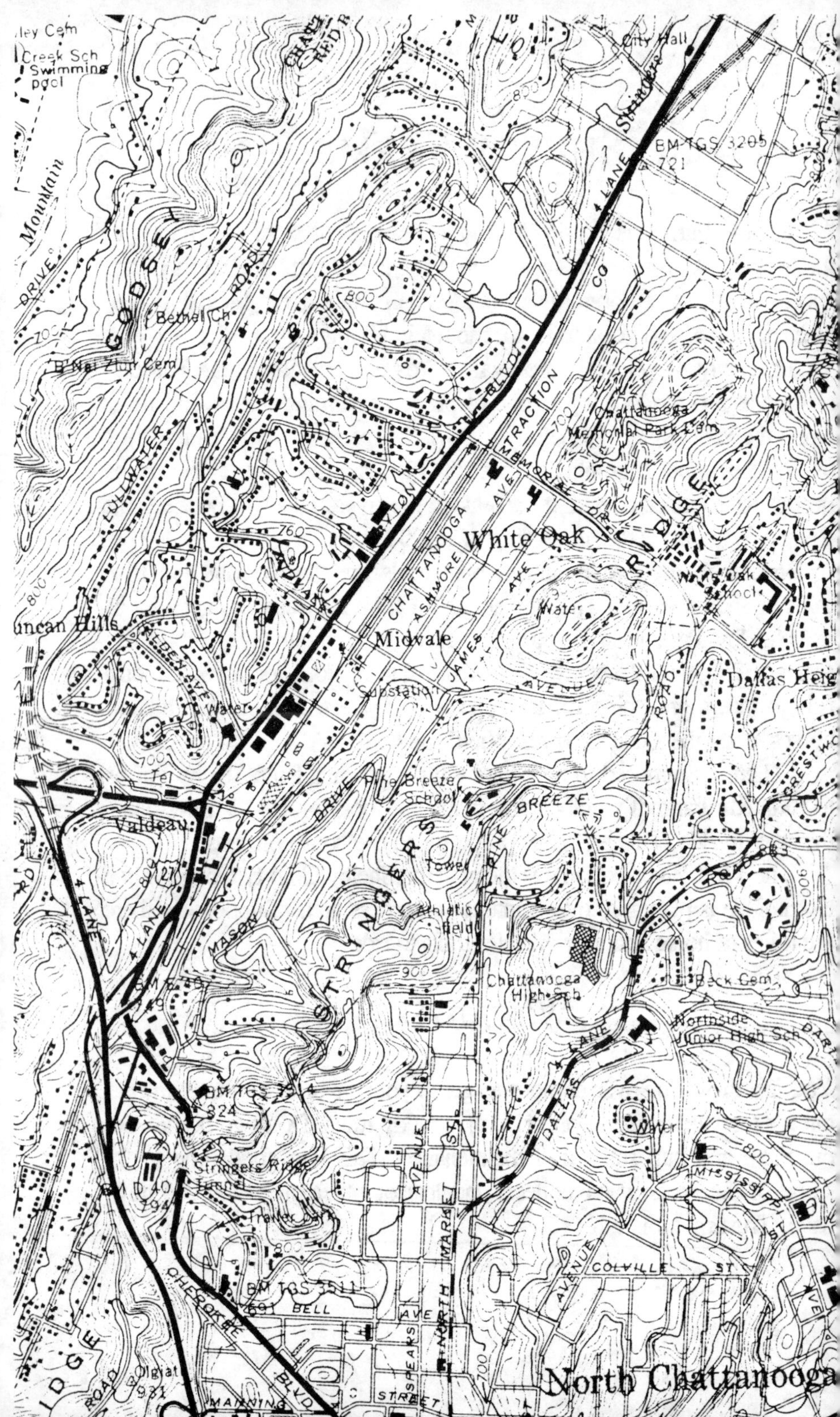
City Hall
Creek Sch
Swimming pool
Mountain
GODSEY
ROAD
Bethel Ch
B'Nai Zion Cem
LULLWATER
Duncan Hills
ALDEN AVE
Water
Tel
Valdeau
4 LANE
MASON
BM TGS 3205
721
4 LANE
CO
TRACTION
BLVD
Chattanooga
Memorial Park Cem
MEMORIAL DR
White Oak
CHATTANOOGA
ASHMORE
AVE
Midvale
JAMES
AVENUE
Substation
Water
School
Dallas Heig
ROAD
CRESTWO
Pine Breeze
School
STRINGERS
DRIVE
PINE
BREEZE
Tower
Athletic Field
Chattanooga
High Sch
Beck Cem
Northside
Junior High Sch
DALLAS
4 LANE
Water
MISSISSIPPI
ST
BM TGS
824
Stringers Ridge
Tunnel
794
Trailer Park
BM TGS 3511
691
BELL
AVE
CHEROKEE
BLVD
NORTH
MARKET
ST
AVENUE
SPEARS
STREET
MANNING
COLVILLE
ST
RIDGE
ROAD
Olgiati
931
North Chattanooga

STRINGER'S RIDGE

Chattanooga riders rejoice: Just a stone's throw from downtown you will find several miles of serious mountain bike riding. Stringer's Ridge is a combination of TVA right of way and an old homestead. You will ride a combination of single track and jeep roads that create a fun and exciting loop.

When you don't have much time or want to get in a quick workout before or after work, this is the place to come. You'll find good steeps to climb and descend and one trail nicknamed Psycho-patch with a fast shoot down the ridge ending with a jump.

Directions: On Cherokee Blvd. going toward town, the road will make a sweeping left turn as you exit the tunnel. At the bottom of the hill turn left at the first road (Bell Street) follow this to the first left, then right again and left up a switch back ridden road to the top of the mountain.

HELPFUL HINTS

Q: What to do when you have a flat tire, but no more patches or a spare tube?

A: Find a grassy area and pack your tire with grass. (This works best with long strands.) You need to pack it as full as possible and try not to get clumps. It's tough to get the wheel back on, so use your tire levers or a quick release lever. I've had to try this on one occasion. It really works!

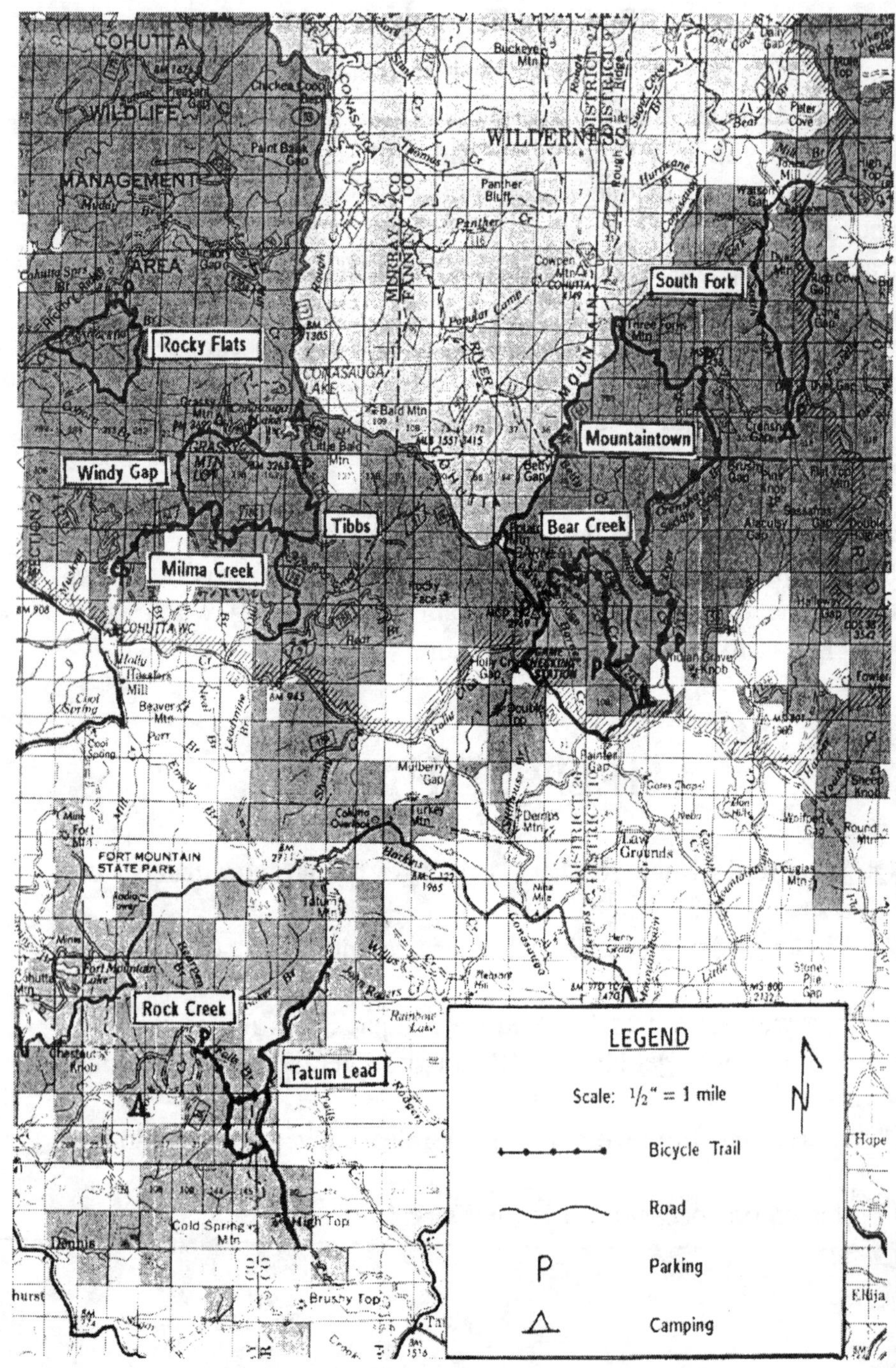

Rocky Flats
Windy Gap
Milma Creek
Tibbs
South Fork
Mountaintown
Bear Creek
Rock Creek
Tatum Lead
COHUTTA
WILDLIFE
MANAGEMENT
AREA
WILDERNESS
CONASAUGA LAKE
FORT MOUNTAIN STATE PARK
LEGEND
Scale: 1/2" = 1 mile
Bicycle Trail
Road
Parking
Camping

TATUM LEAD / ROCK CREEK, GA

This is just another of the excellent trails to ride when in the Bear Creek area. Tatum Lead is actually quite different from other trails in the area. It is an old logging road that runs along the ridge of Tatum Mountain. You ride through dense hardwood and pine forests, weaving in and out along ridge after ridge. Probably the biggest highlight besides the scenery are the banked turns that are just begging to be run without touching the brakes.

The first two miles is a right-of-way across private land and is mostly gravel. Once you enter the National Forest, you'll be on the main trail. Tatum Lead is a moderate seven-mile trip out and back.

You can make this an interesting and much more difficult ride if you wish. The Rock Creek Loop takes off about three or four miles into your ride. This was the trail that inspired the "Big Air in North Georgia" story from my riding buddy Sam Poyner. If you have the heart for a 40-minute grunt of a climb, you'll be rewarded with one of the steepest, non-ending, bike-launching trips in the world! To eliminate erosion, there are three-foot waterbars, one after the other all the way down the mountain. It is a blast. To get the maximum fun from Rock Creek you need to go down the second trail. It is actually a loop that connects both ends to Tatum. We have never actually seen a trail sign, but there are only two branches off of Tatum Lead. Turn right on the second one and hang on to your brakes.

We have never ridden down to Rock Creek, but you will see the split where you can turn right and make the *big* climb back up to Tatum, or stay straight and ride to the parking area for Rock Creek.

Directions to Tatum Lead: From Chatsworth, take U.S. 52 east about 11.3 miles. The trail head will be on your right, and you can park there. Once you pass the overlook, it's about a mile farther and starts as a gravel road.

Directions to Rock Creek: From Chatsworth, take U. S. 52 east about one mile. Turn right onto the Old Federal Road for about four miles. Turn left at the sign to Peeples Lake/Rock Creek Trail. Follow this gravel road 5.9 miles to the parking area.

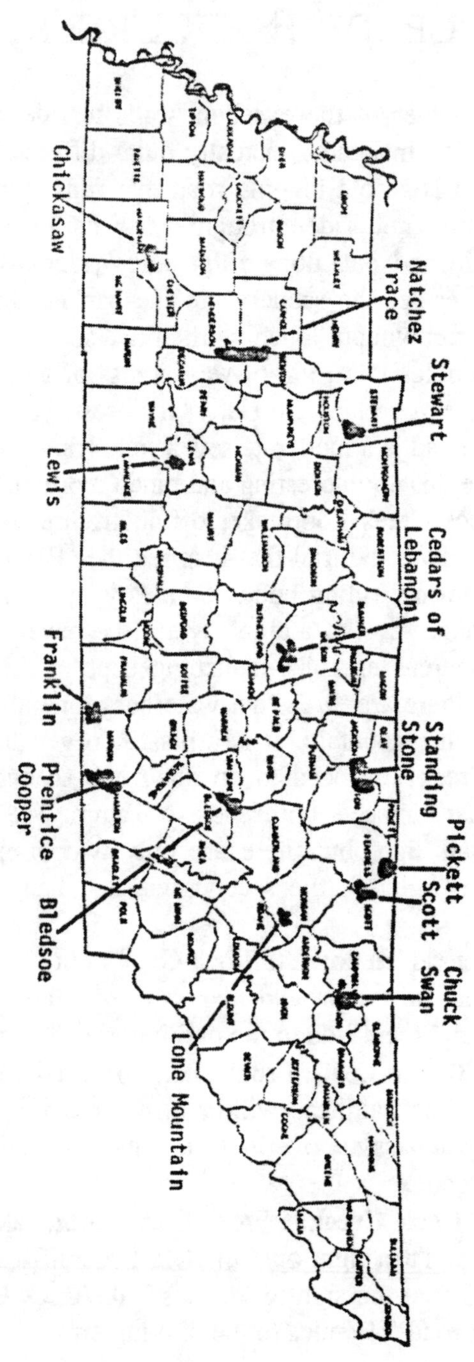
Chickasaw
Natchez Trace
Stewart
Lewis
Cedars of Lebanon
Franklin
Standing Stone
Prentice Cooper
Pickett
Scott
Chuck Swan
Bledsoe
Lone Mountain

TENNESSEE STATE FORESTS

Throughout Tennessee, the Department of Conservation manages nearly 150,000 acres of land set aside "to provide for the multiple-use management of the various renewable and non-renewable resources such that those resources are utilized in the combination that best meets the needs of the people of Tennessee." There are 13 individual forests throughout the state which serve many purposes including recreation. We are allowed to ride in all State Forests, excluding any designated State Parks. The following is a listing of the State Forests in Tennessee:

Bledsoe State Forest. (6,656 acres). Tom Hudlow, 615-775-0251.

Cedars of Lebanon S.F. (6,943 acres). Gerald Eaton, 615-790-0198. See page 30-31.

Chickasaw S.F. (13,104 acres). Roy Ward, 901-989-5252. See page 40 - 41.

Chuck Swan S.F. (24,399 acres). David Arnold, 423-278-3348. See page 26.

Franklin S.F. (6,941 acres). Clint Stromeier, 615-967-0757. See page 53 - 55.

Lewis S.F. (1,257 acres). Len Womack, 615-729-3535.

Lone Mountain S.F. (3,597 acres). Brant Miller, 423-354-0258. See pages 72 - 73.

Natchez Trace S.F. (35,904 acres). Gary Roark, 901-968-4541. See pages 78 - 81

Pickett S.F. (10,887 acres). Billy Swafford, 615-484-4227.

Prentice Cooper S.F. (23,759 acres). Kelly Jenkins, 423-949-3821. See page 99 - 101.

Scott S.F. (3,182 acres). Rick Walker, 423-562-7838.

Standing Stone S.F. (8,455 acres). 423-526-9502.

Stewart S.F. (4,000 acres). Mike Huddleston, 615-552-3909.

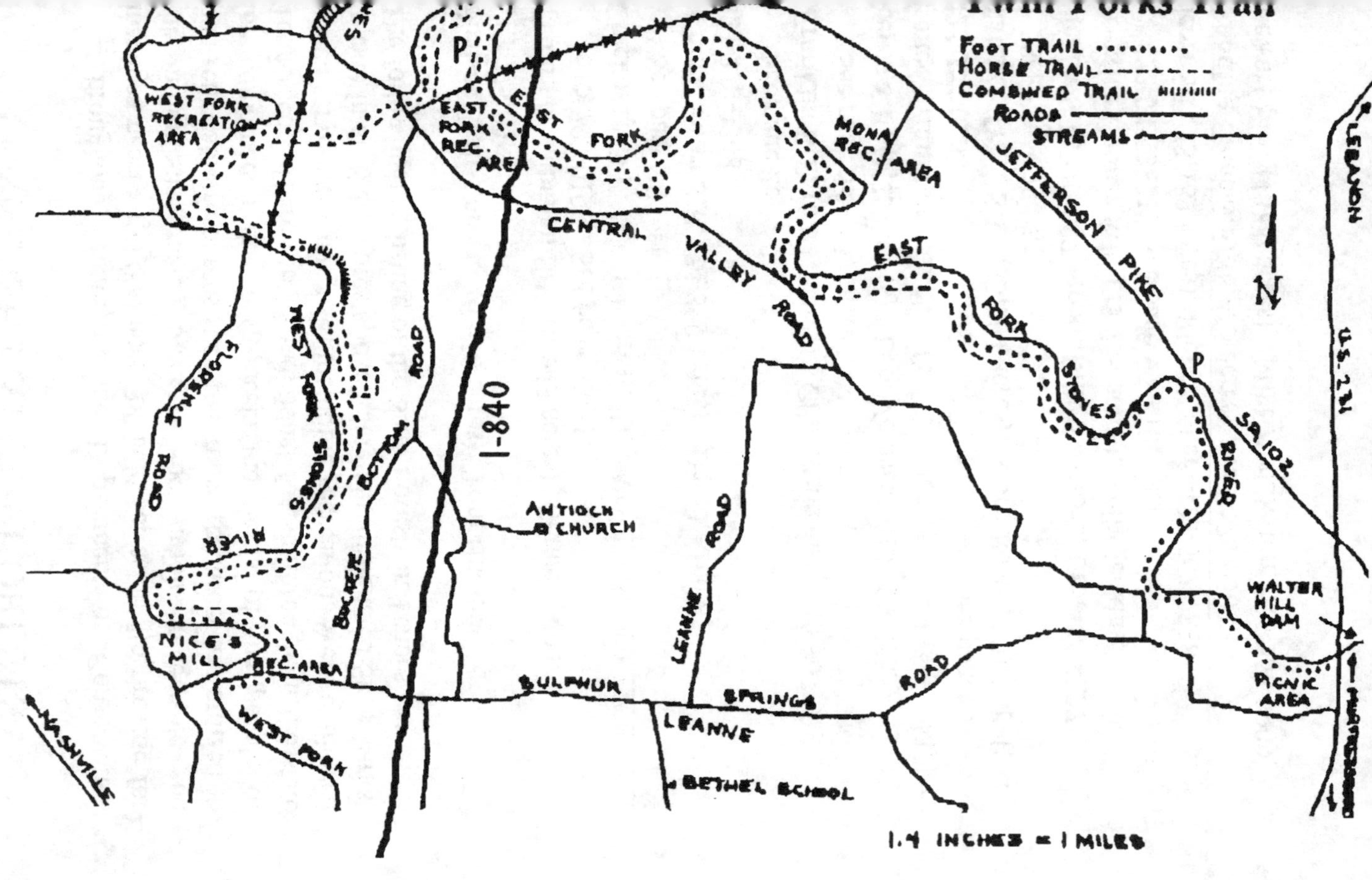
FOOT TRAIL
HORSE TRAIL
COMBINED TRAIL
ROADS
STREAMS
WEST FORK RECREATION AREA
P
EAST FORK REC. AREA
EAST FORK
MONA REC. AREA
JEFFERSON PIKE
LEBANON
CENTRAL VALLEY ROAD
EAST FORK STONES RIVER
N
U.S. 231
SR 102
FLORENCE ROAD
WEST FORK STONES RIVER
BUCKEYE BOTTOM ROAD
I-840
ANTIOCH CHURCH
LEANNE ROAD
WALTER HILL DAM
NICE'S MILL REC. AREA
SULPHUR SPRINGS ROAD
PICNIC AREA
LEANNE
NASHVILLE
WEST FORK
BETHEL SCHOOL
1.4 INCHES = 1 MILES

TWIN FORKS TRAIL

The Twin Forks trail is a multi-use trail that runs along the east and west forks of the Stones River north of Murfreesboro. All together there are more than 10 miles of rideable trails to explore, most of which would be rated as easy. That means beginner and intermediate riders have yet another place to explore without having to struggle on a difficult trail.

There are a number of starting points. To start on the south end of the trail, turn left on Sulphur Springs Road, take the first right on Central Valley, and park where the road makes a sharp left turn. The horse trail leads north from the turn in the road. From that point on the riding is quite easy and scenic. You also can park at the East Fork Recreation Area. Take the trail leading south from the parking lot, under the bridge. When you reach the gravel road, turn left and the trail will lead through a field. Follow the gravel trail to the top of the hill, then follow the dirt trail to the right.

You will notice from the map that there is also a hiking trail that parallels the horse trail. Try to avoid riding on it if possible. It is much more difficult and requires carrying your bike in many places. At times you will not be sure which is which, generally the horse trail stays along the top of the ridge. The river is always nearby and wildlife is extremely abundant.

Trails are mainly wide singletrack with a few gravel roads. The trail is quite muddy when wet. I don't recommend riding here if the ground is saturated. Remember this is a horse trail so be prepared for rough trails during peak riding season. This also means you should be aware of horses you may encounter during your ride. Dismount and let them pass.

This is a WMA and Corps of Engineers property. Trail maintenance has been sketchy, most recently (fall, '96) they were in great shape. I believe this is the finest beginner/intermediate trail in Middle TN. The scenery is terrific, it's convenient and you can make a good 20-mile ride out of it. There are several shortcuts too.

Directions: Walter Hill Dam is located five miles north of Murfreesboro on Hwy. 231. It is 23 miles south of Lebanon.

Don't take land access for granted. Mountain biking is a new sport, and your actions on your next ride will influence which trails will be open for bicycle use in the years to come. Minimizing skidding, avoiding muddy areas, and being courteous to hikers and equestrians are simple things we can all do on every ride to keep the land open to bicycles. And if you're feeling ambitious, voluntary trail maintenance and packing out others' trash will benefit everyone.

The International Mountain Bicycling Association (IMBA) has established these rules for good trail riding:

- Ride on open trails only
- Leave no trace
- Control your bicycle
- Always yield the trail
- Never spook animals
- Plan ahead

Remember, good trail habits are everyone's business. For more information contact IMBA at P.O. Box 412043, Los Angeles, CA, 90041. Or call IMBA at 1-818/792-8830.

the dirt clods™
BY CURT EVANS

MOUNTAIN BIKERS NEED TO SHARE THE RESPONSIBILITY OF TRAIL MAINTENANCE.

AS MEMBERS OF THE 'TRAIL FAMILY,' WE NEED TO CONTRIBUTE TO THE UPKEEP AND REBUILDING OF TRAILS.

OCCASIONALLY WE HAVE TO SACRIFICE RIDING TIME AND PUT IN SOME HARD WORK AND SWEAT.

TRAIL WORK BUILDS TRUST WITH OTHER OUTDOOR USERS, IMPRESSES LAND MANAGERS, AND PREVENTS EROSION...

AWESOME WHOOPS!
KILLER JUMP!
PLUS, TRAIL BUILDING HAS A FEW SIDE BENEFITS!
WICKED BERM!
©1994 CURT EVANS

WILDLIFE MANAGEMENT AREAS

Throughout Tennessee, 73 W.M.A.s are managed by the Tennessee Wildlife Resources Agency. These areas vary in size from 88 to 625,000 acres. Although the state manages this land, all the money needed to purchase and run these units comes solely from the sale of hunting and fishing licenses. This land is first and foremost for the hunters. **WE ARE NOT ALLOWED IN TENNESSEE'S W.M.A.'s DURING BIG GAME OR TURKEY SEASON.**

These are the areas with more than 2,000 acres:

AEDC, Coffee/Franklin Counties. Archie Whitehead, 615-967-6101. (32,000 acres). Not behind closed gates.

Anderson-Tully, Lauderdale County. Willis Wheeler, 901-635-2475 (11,000 acres). See page 122.

Camden Unit, Benton County. Robert Wheat, 901-593-3332 (3,682 acres).

Catoosa, Cumberland/Morgan Counties. John Hamby 423-484-4094 (79,740 acres). See page 27.

Cheatham, Cheatham County. Randy Comer, 615-792-4510 (20,818 acres). See page 33.

Cherokee, Cherokee National Forest. (625,000 acres) See pages 36 - 37.

Chickamauga, Bradley/McMinn/Rhea/Meigs/Hamilton Cty.s. Carl Campbell, 423-339-2161 (4,000 acres). See page 37.

Chickasaw, Hardeman/Chester Co. (11,215 acres). See pg. 40.

Chilhowee Mountain, Blount/Sevier Counties. (6,000 acres).

Chuck Swan, Union/Campbell Counties. (24,444 acres) Phil Bledsoe, 423-278-3248 See page 26.

Cordell Hull, Jackson/Smith Counties. (25,000 acres). Gary Black, 615-858-2995.

Cumberland Springs, Moore County. (6,079 acres).

Doe Mountain, Johnson County. (8,300 acres).

Eagle Creek, Wayne County. (22,000 acres).

Fall Creek Falls, Bledsoe County. (7,000 acres). See page 48.

Gallatin Steam Plant, Sumner County (2,200 acres).

Gooch, Obion County. (7,000 acres). Ralph Gray, 901-536-0687

Land Between the Lakes, Stewart County. (180,000 acres). 502-924-5603. See page 66.

Laurel Hill, Lawrence County. (14,000 acres). Gene White, 615-762-2079

Moss Island, Dyer County. (3,400 acres). Alan Peterson, 901-423-5725

Mt. Roosevelt, Cumberland/Roane/Morgan Co. (11,000 acres).

Natchez Trace, Benton/Carroll/Henderson County (48,000 acres). Larry Dickson, 901-876-8764. See page 78.

Obion River, Obion/Weakley/Gibson Counties. (7,000 acres). Ralph Gray 901-536-0687

Prentice Cooper, Marion County. (24,000 acres). Dan Lavacot, 615-658-2726. See page 99.

Reelfoot, Lake/Obion Counties. (24,000 acres). Paul Brown, 901-253-7841.

Royal Blue, Campbell/Scott Counties. (43,000 acres). Stan Stooksbury, 615-566-8557.

Shelby Forest, Shelby County. (13,000 acres). Dan Fuqua, 901-876-5169.

Standing Stone, Overton County. (8,764 acres).

Tellico Lake, Monroe County (6,000 acres) David Whitehead, 423-884-6767.

Watts Bar, Roane County, (5,480 acres). Carl Campbell, 423-339-2161.

West Sandy, Henry County. (4,319 acres). Robert Wheat, 901-593-3332.

White Oak, Hardin County (6,000). Jeff Joyner, 901-687-3444.

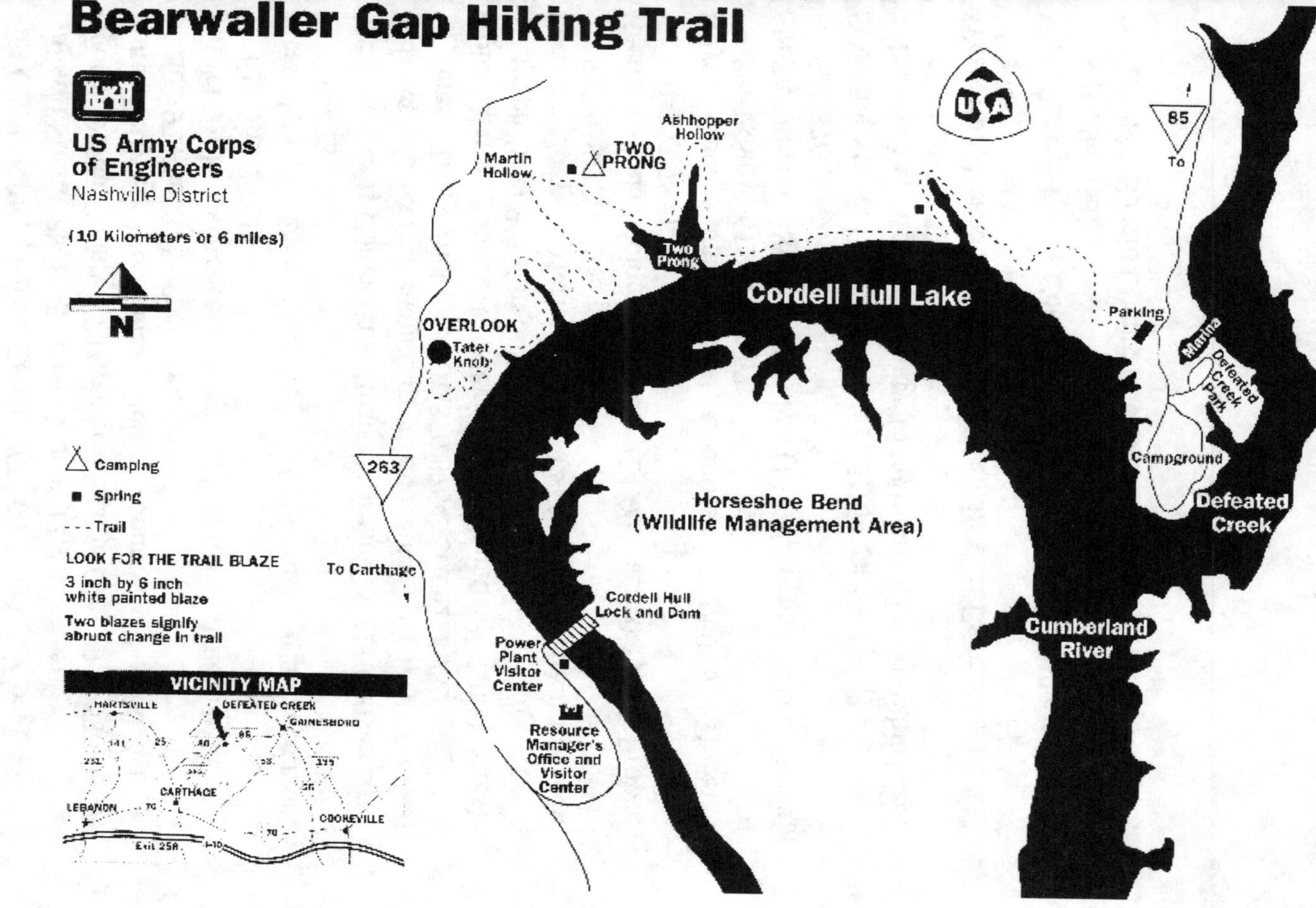
Bearwaller Gap Hiking Trail
US Army Corps
of Engineers
Nashville District
(10 Kilometers or 6 miles)
N
Camping
Spring
- - - Trail
LOOK FOR THE TRAIL BLAZE
3 inch by 6 inch
white painted blaze
Two blazes signify
abrupt change in trail
VICINITY MAP
HARTSVILLE
DEFEATED CREEK
GAINESBORO
CARTHAGE
LEBANON
COOKEVILLE
Exit 258
I-40
263
To Carthage
OVERLOOK
Tater
Knob
Martin
Hollow
TWO
PRONG
Ashhopper
Hollow
Two
Prong
Cordell Hull Lake
Horseshoe Bend
(Wildlife Management Area)
Cordell Hull
Lock and Dam
Power
Plant
Visitor
Center
Resource
Manager's
Office and
Visitor
Center
Cumberland
River
85
To
Parking
Marina
Defeated
Creek
Park
Campground
Defeated
Creek

BEARWALLER GAP

Yikes! This place is tough. If you're not familiar with the phrases "I'm sick of carrying my bike" or "%#*@ that's a nasty section", this is not for you. Located 80 miles east of Nashville, this small but deadly hiking trail was officially opened to us early in `97. I found it with a random phone call and claim the first mountain bike ascent on Tater Knob. If you are an advanced rider, tired of the same old thing and are looking for a true adventure, Bearwaller Gap will satisfy the need.

The fun starts 50 yards into the woods. You are greeted with a steep, rocky climb that is unrideable in many sections. The following downhill is even steeper with lots of ledges and sharp switch-backs. Plan on lots of hiking on the first section, but it gets better. (Resist the temptation to turn around or leave your bike and hike.) The next section along the lake is more climbing, but it's rideable and there are several overlooks for a quick rest. A fun technical downhill into Ashhopper Hollow leads to a rutted, rocky four-wheeler road that you follow for about 200 yards, then it's just a rocky jeep road.

When you reach the Two Prong camping area, you're done with the jeep road, and it's back to singletrack when you reach the top of the next ridge. This is a primitive camp, with a spring, outhouse and picnic table. The next mile is quite rideable, though technical with a challenging downhill. Now it's time to start up to Tater Knob. There has been some horse traffic here so many of the steep sections are unrideable. This is the longest climb and there's lots of hiking, but you are rewarded at the top with a beautiful overlook of the lake and Cordell Hull Dam.

You can backtrack on the trail home or a 20-minute road ride brings you back to the parking area. Again, if you are not a highly advanced rider with technical skills you will not like this trail. Plan on two hours one-way (six miles). Bring tools--it's a good place to break something.

Directions: Access is easy and well marked. From I-40, exit at Carthage on Hwy. 25 and drive north through town. Turn right on Hwy. 263 and follow it over the dam. You will pass Tater Knob then meet Hwy. 85. Turn right for 2 miles, turn right into Defeated Creek Park and Campground. There is a beach and restrooms are available.

West Tennessee Areas

Anderson-Tully W.M.A.

Located south of the Chickasaw Refuge, Anderson Tully has 11,000 acres of land for hunters and recreational users. Most of the land is wooded, and logging trails are available.

Directions: From Covington, drive north on Hwy. 51, then left on Hwy. 87 past the Ft. Pillow Prison. Crutcher Lake Road will lead you to the headquarters.

Chickasaw National Wildlife Refuge

Located eight miles east of Ripley, Chickasaw N.W.R. offers 20,000 acres of wooded terrain to ride. There are some main roads throughout the area and logging roads running all over the place. Some of the land is swampy so beware. The Mississippi runs along the west side of the park, and large peninsulas are available to ride. **Directions:** From Ripley, take Hwy. 19 West to Barr Road. It runs through the middle of the Refuge. For more information, call Randy Cook at 901-635-7621.

Hatchie National Wildlife Refuge

This is a huge area just south of Brownsville. The Refuge is only 11,000 acres, but when you add in the Hatchie Bottoms, you can really put together a long ride. There are gravel roads throughout the area, some of which are closed occasionally due to flooding. You'll also find a variety of additional trails to explore running along the Hatchie River.

Directions: Take I-40 East from Memphis to exit 52. Go north on Hwy. 75, and the main entrance will be a couple miles up the road. For more information, call Marvin Nichols at 901-722-0501.

Meeman Shelby Forest

Here you will find 12,500 acres of land overlooking the Mississippi River. I am not sure of the specific trail situation, however there is a good supply of jeep and fire roads to explore. The hiking trails are off limits, although I've been told it is worth the hike up for a spectacular view of the river from the bluffs.

Located just 13 miles north of Memphis, this should provide a popular place to ride if you are courteous to other users.

Directions: Take North Watkins up to Locke Road. Turn left and you will enter the park.

HELPFUL HINTS

Poison Ivy

1. *Scratching the blister spreads the rash.*
   False- The rash is sparked by contact with a colorless oil called urushiol found on the plant's leaves and stem. Only by touching this oil will you spread the rash.

2. *You can catch poison ivy from someone else.*
   False- The rash can't travel from person to person. Only direct contact with the oil causes the rash.

3. *Water inactivates the oil.*
   True- When you think you've been in contact, remember to rinse off your legs and arms in the next stream you cross.

4. If the rash does not go away within 3 or 4 days, see a doctor. A steroid shot will clear it up quickly.

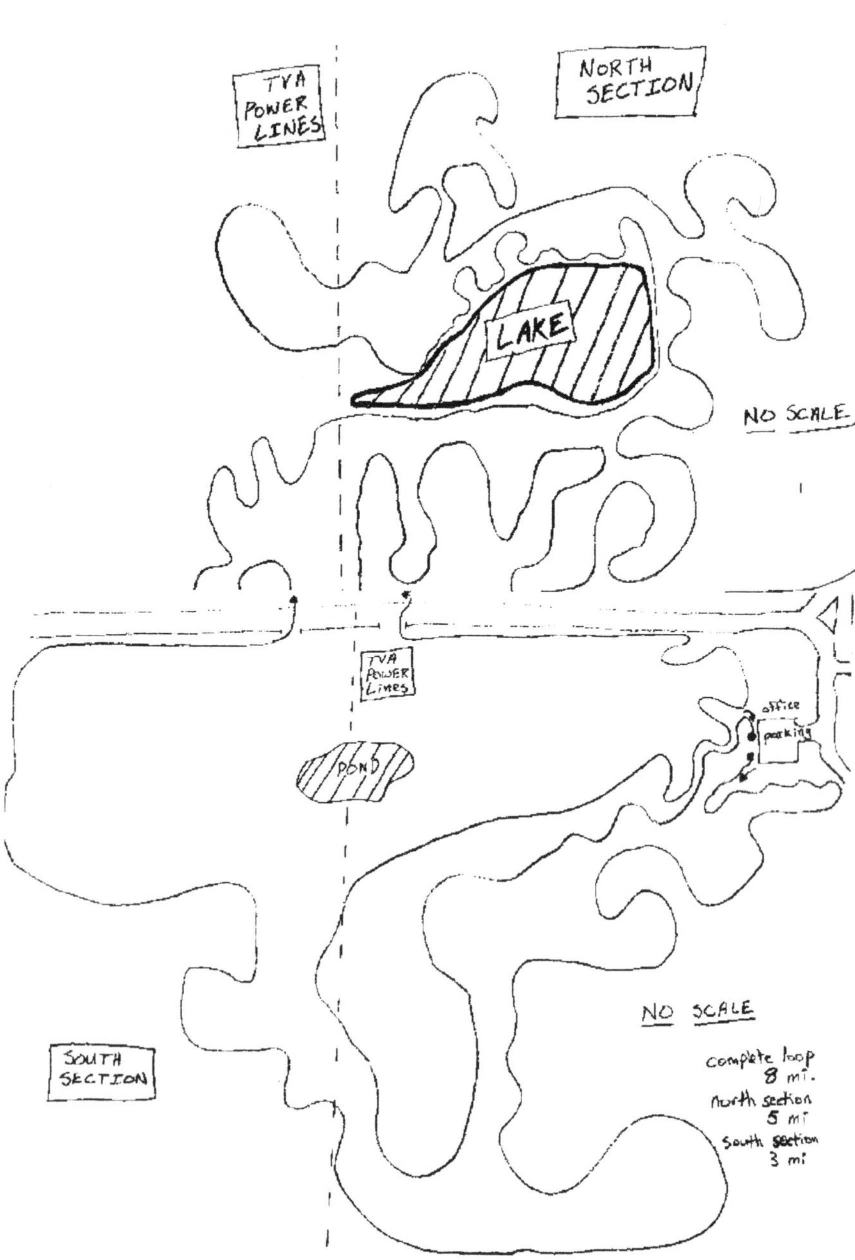
TVA POWER LINES
NORTH SECTION
LAKE
NO SCALE
TVA POWER Lines
office
parking
POND
NO SCALE
complete loop 8 mi.
north section 5 mi
South section 3 mi
SOUTH SECTION

YOUTH TOWN

The Youth Town trail is a seven-mile forested single-track loop located on private property south of Jackson, TN. The clearly marked trail features strenuous climbs, fast downhills, rolling sections and technical obstacles. The single-track changes quickly from open passing areas to twisting, narrow sections of hard pack and loose soil. Scenery changes from hardwood forest to open pasture land and includes the circumference of an 18 acre lake.

The trail is privately maintained by the Tred-Heads Mountain Bike Club, who host spring and fall NORBA races. Ample parking, drinking water and a bike wash area are available at the trail head.

Permits are required for all riders and are available by filling out a one-time application at the trail office adjacent to the trail head. A $10 annual fee is used for trail maintenance and improvements. After a permit has been issued, riders may use the trail freely during daylight hours, seven days per week.

Directions: The trail head is located six miles south of Jackson, TN, just off U.S. Highway 45. From Jackson, turn right at the Youth Town of Tennessee sign, two miles after the highway turns into a divided 4-lane. After turning follow the "Mountain Bike Trail" signs to the parking area and office. For more information contact, Steve Tillerous at Summit Quest, 901-988-5207.

About the author

Although David Moore has always enjoyed the outdoors, it wasn't until the spring of 1990 that he realized the enjoyment and fun one can experience from riding through the woods on a bicycle. Working as a regional account director in the early 90s provided David the opportunity to travel throughout Tennessee and to ride most of the known and unknown off-road trails. Three years later, with a car full of topo maps and many memories, he decided to share his adventures with other riders around the state, and he began to write this book.

David is a past president of the Sumner County Cycle Club and a member of many other cycling clubs. He is also a member of IMBA and works diligently to teach the "Rules of the Trail." Promoting recreational rides and races through the SCCC provides many opportunities to explore new areas of the state.

In the real world, David works as a financial advisor for The Capital Financial Group selling insurance and investments in Nashville, TN. He works with families and small business owners in the areas of investment and estate planning, tax reduction, business continuation and employee benefits. As a Registered Representative, he is responsible for helping clients design proper portfolio allocations to reduce risk and increase returns. If you have questions about financial planning, contact him at 615-824-4845.

NOTES

NOTES